Intuitive
Self-Healing

Intuitive
Self-Healing

Achieve Balance and Wellness
Through the Body's Energy Centers

Marie Manuchehri, RN

sounds true
BOULDER, COLORADO

Sounds True, Inc.
Boulder, CO 80306

© 2012 Marie Manuchehri

Published 2012, 2019

Illustrations © 2012 Susan Russell Hall
Cover and book design by Rachael Murray
Author photo by Heather B. Allison
Cover photo © Kati Molin, shutterstock.com

Disclaimer:
The advice given in this book is not meant to be a substitute for sound
medical advice. The author appreciates and honors all forms of medicine
and recommends that all clients and readers maintain regular healthcare
visits with a qualified health practitioner.

To protect privacy, some client names have been changed.

Printed in the United States of America

Library of Congress Cataloging-in-Publication Data

Manuchehri, Marie.
Intuitive self-healing: achieve balance and wellness through the body's
energy centers / Marie Manuchehri.
     p. cm.
Includes bibliographical references.
ISBN 978-1-60407-627-1
1. Intuition. 2. Mind and body therapies. 3. Mental healing. 4. Chakras.
I. Title.
RZ999.M345 2012
615.5--dc23
2011033904

eBook ISBN: 978-1-60407-751-3

10 9 8 7 6

To the human race, especially my daughters
Maryam, Misha, and Mina

I love you all.

I'M GRATEFUL TO BE PART of the growing and ever-changing field of energy medicine. I find human beings *amazing,* and the human condition fascinating. I believe we are all gifted and talented beyond our wildest dreams.

Contents

Acknowledgments

I GIVE MY DEEPEST THANKS to the many people who supported me in writing this book.

To my writing coach, Emily Warn, who helped me finish a book I had been dreaming of completing for years. Emily, your love of teaching and writing is a winning combination. Your ability to teach me that I can write changed my world.

To Susie Russell Hall, for her amazing illustrations. Your skill and insight breathed life into the pages of this book.

To my dear friends and children Andria Friesen, Trish Maharam, Timothy Brodesser, Amy Gunter, Sheila Dunn Merritt, Maryam Manuchehri, Misha Manuchehri, and Mina Manuchehri, for tirelessly reading and rereading the book's chapters. Your feedback and enthusiasm helped me enormously.

To my kind assistant, Elissa Wildenborg, who kept all the balls in the air so I could write.

To my agent, Eric Myers, for helping me acquire the publisher of my dreams.

To Ainslie MacLeod, a very special thank you for your friendship, intuition, and support.

And finally, thank you to my clients, who didn't stop asking me to write a book. It has been my greatest pleasure.

Introduction

FALL 1997: BEGINNINGS

Hundreds of tiny golden pyramids, each about one inch in diameter, spin around my bed, humming and vibrating softly. Glowing brightly, they illuminate the bedroom just before dawn, allowing me to see their tiny mud-brick structure— a vision that has been appearing for several weeks. Their vibration pulses through my body, as if they are alive and teaching me their rhythm. I hold still between the warm white sheets, worried that the throbbing hum will wake my slumbering husband next to me and our daughters down the hall. My husband doesn't stir. Then I remember—only I can see, hear, and feel the pyramids.

This vision was only one in a series of mystical encounters that had begun months before. The morning greeting answered my nightly question: would the triangles disappear as abruptly as they appeared?

The paranormal experiences were a welcome distraction from my predictable suburban life: kids, work, grocery shopping, cooking, and cleaning. Their unexplained wonder gave me something to look forward to, something just for me. They also reminded me of my childhood home. As a teenager, I would avidly read the books on spirituality and self-actualization that filled my mother's bookshelves. They awakened something in me that I couldn't explain but that touched my heart deeply. On Sundays I visited churches, searching for human contact that could move me as these books did. I found none. I kept my activities secret from my peer group, hoping to fit in. Now, years later, what I remembered from my reading allowed me to trust these auditory and visual encounters that were not of this world.

During this time I worked as a registered oncology nurse, an odd career choice given my holistic upbringing; in my childhood home we would often eat organic food and take nutritional supplements, and we saw a chiropractor as our primary physician. I loved nursing, though, but worried that if a patient required an emergency intervention such as a defibrillator to restart the heart, the mystical images, voices, and feelings that I sometimes perceived might distract me. I sensed my inner awareness changing and wondered if I would easily recognize signs of distress and respond quickly with a crash cart.

I decided to share my worries with my supervisor, Lois Williams. When she saw me walking toward her second-floor office, she waved me in. I often visited her office to request additional support for treatments that were outside of routine hospital protocol. She was always helpful and interested in my opinions, and she often came up with creative solutions. Lois probably thought I was visiting for a similar reason this time. I was pretty sure she had never dealt with this type of problem.

I told Lois about the golden pyramids, the odd feelings, and the voices I'd been hearing. Her physical response was calm and centered. I had no idea what she was thinking.

Surprisingly, she neither suspended me from my job nor ordered a psychiatric evaluation. Instead, she explained that I was viewing energy. She encouraged me to touch patients with my hands instead of a stethoscope. Terms such as *chakra* and *hands-on healing* flowed from her mouth as if they were common to her vocabulary. I had no idea what a chakra was, but hearing the word set in motion a constant wave of emotion in my heart. As I backed out of her office in disbelief about our conversation, I saw for the first time a calming waterfall behind her desk. Behind the waterfall was a beautifully framed picture of an angel, who seemed to smile.

Three days later, the wave in my chest—as I could think of little else—enticed me to lay my hands on a patient. Not knowing what would happen, I carefully chose the healthiest patient on the floor, a sixty-year-old female scheduled to go home the next day. Having no clue about what to do, I entered her hospital room and promptly shut the door behind me, hoping to prevent anyone else from coming in and asking me what I was doing. I introduced myself to the patient. Her face was tight; she probably thought I had a needle or some other invasive tool to prod her with. I explained that I wanted to gently place my hands on her. Her face softened as my words sank in. She liked the idea. I paused, stunned: my multisensory world frightened no one.

Even though I had touched hundreds of patients as a nurse, this time felt different. A strange inner calm filled my body as I gently laid my hands on top of the cotton hospital blanket, near the middle of the woman's belly. She closed her eyes and softly sighed. My eyes shut, too. Was it my focus on the simple act of touching another that relaxed us? In seconds I heard a high-pitched, barely audible harp melody. The haunting tune flooded my senses, coming from a place that was familiar, but of which I had no conscious memory. The unknown yet tangible surroundings and the melodic music brought tears down my cheeks. Blushing, I peeked with one moist eye at the patient. Her eyes were still closed. She, too, was freely weeping. It seemed as if the patient and I stayed in a magical state for hours, but when I gazed at the clock on the wall, only a few minutes had passed.

Suddenly I felt my head pulled intensely toward her body, forcing my eyes wide open. I was within inches of her, looking directly at her midsection. Panic rose in me as the force became stronger. I turned my head slightly to look at the patient. Her calm, tear-stained face had not changed. Seeing her peaceful look settled me. What was I afraid of? My mind gave me a quick pep talk: *Something wonderful is happening, just go with it.*

I lowered my head a few inches closer to her stomach, relaxing the strained muscles in my neck, and closed my eyes. An image of the woman I was touching appeared, just as alive as she was. In my mind, I could see her chest rise and fall, her eyelids slightly flutter, and her left foot move underneath the white blanket.

I wanted to open my eyes to see if what I was viewing was simultaneously happening in the room, but then the vision changed. Strangely and miraculously, I was now viewing the inside of the patient's body. As if I were watching the Discovery Channel, I could see her organs, tissues, bones, and blood pulsating together. I momentarily felt gratitude for the anatomy classes I'd taken years ago. Had they been in preparation for this event?

A new vision replaced my wandering thoughts. Many colored balls, or orbs, lined the center of her body: a yellow ball of light in her abdomen, a white glow at the top of her head, and a radiant green ball deep in the center of her chest. The orbs were just as alive as her veins and arteries. And just as quickly the spheres changed shape, forming beautiful cones spinning deep within her body. More spinning lights ran down her body. I felt as if I were watching a psychedelic light show.

At the same time, other information about her life was relayed to me. It was not expressed in the way that you hear words, yet the information was similar. A whirlwind of facts kept coming: childhood illness, a marriage, and other adult relationships, all of which somehow related to the onset of adult health issues. My mind raced to keep up but was incapable of remembering it all. As if the cones knew of my inability, the information abruptly stopped. I almost hooted with the rush, but before I could make a sound, a new sensation shocked me—a faint human touch on the top of my hands. The patient was rubbing them and smiling, signaling that we were done.

SUMMER 2010: ENERGY MEDICINE AT WORK

After that day, more than anything, I wanted to lay my hands on people to help them heal. In the hospital, I asked hundreds of patients for permission to do so. Only one said no. I approached patients who weren't assigned to me so that I wouldn't know their diagnoses. I compared my energy readings with their medical charts. Over time, through the realization of my accuracy, I built a dictionary in my mind of what the impressions meant. With every new patient I touched, stronger energies pulsed through my body, improving my ability to retain the stories that their bodies shared—information that led me to understand the emotional reasons for their illnesses.

I now know that the spinning balls of light that I viewed during my first encounter and with other patients in the hospital are called chakras—beautiful energy centers in the body that transmit and receive life energy. Each chakra has its own color and unique role in maintaining vitality in your body, mind, and spirit. Chakras are multidimensional, appearing round or cone-shaped. They form the main centers of a system that contains thousands of smaller energy points. The term chakra is a Sanskrit word meaning wheel or disc. Descriptions of the chakras first appeared in the Vedas, ancient spiritual texts dating back to 2,000 BC. This complex circuitry holds within it the keys to our evolution and wholeness.

I had hoped to continue using my skills in the hospital and perhaps teach them to other nurses. I soon realized that the traditional hospitals weren't yet ready for that type of change. If I wanted to focus on energy medicine, I would need to start a private practice. Today I treat thousands of people worldwide from all walks of life and in every age group.

I've written this book because I want to share with you, the reader, what I've discovered over the past thirteen years about the energetics of healing. My experiences have taught me more than I thought I could learn in a lifetime—astonishing truths about human beings: how our consciousness, love, and recognition of our illusions can work together to help us heal.

In this book, you will read real-life client stories and view beautiful illustrations that will help you learn about the chakra system and understand more fully that everything is energy. You will also recognize that modern medicine's tools for healing, such as surgery and pharmacology, although necessary, are limited. Energy medicine's tools are boundless and life changing. Combining conventional medicine or

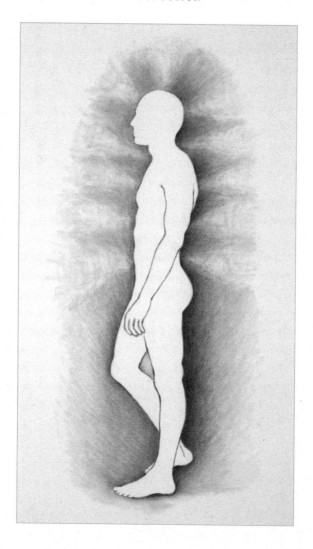

FIGURE 1. *Each of the seven primary chakras receives and transmits vital life-force energy through a spinning motion. The chakras send energy into the body and send illumination beyond the body.*

holistic medicine with energy medicine can speed a person's body toward lasting health. Truly, everyone has the power to change their reality and create a vital, fulfilling, and healthy life. Self-awareness is the key to making the changes, and energy medicine can help you get there.

At the end of each chapter, you'll find easy-to-follow energy medicine exercises that I recommend to all my clients because I believe that each person is his or her own best healer. I derived the exercises from childhood experiences, my energy medicine practice, yoga, and from a popular 1960's psychological therapy called Core Energetic. These exercises can positively change energy (physical, emotional, mental, and spiritual) within seconds. They release stagnant energy from a chakra and its surrounding anatomical area, while increasing vital energy flowing into the body. Some of these exercises take very little time, approximately one minute each. They may be a little unusual, but they work amazingly well!

May this book inspire healing in every area of your life!

Joyful blessings,
Marie

Intuitive Self-Healing

INTUITIVE HEALING ISN'T NEW. IT'S been around for centuries, but we have forgotten what it means to listen to our own body's messages. Instead, we have given our healing power away by not paying attention to our feelings and centered thoughts when we feel ill or are diagnosed with a disease. Intuition by definition is about knowing. Intuitive healing begins with discovering the vital energy within. There is nothing unusual about it. We all possess it. Each of us is our own best healer.

Coming to know this intelligence within manifests itself in many different ways. Some people view images in their mind, hear words, or feel sensations. Others pick up insights during their daily life which seem to come from others—from radio, television, or billboard advertisements. Wherever our insights arise from, we all possess the aptitude to recognize them and discover what is in our best interest.

Even if you have tried many times to perceive your internal messages, but feel that you possess no skill to do so—trust me you do. After working with thousands of clients, I've learned that everyone has the capacity to receive, interpret, and successfully use their senses. You have this ability because we are genuinely powerful. You might be unaware of your great fortune, but nevertheless you are powerful.

More people are beginning to understand personal power, but it remains a new concept. Individual power is limitless and we can learn to utilize it through internal awareness. Yet, somehow we feel that we don't have this authority over our own lives, and in particular over our bodies. Instead, we make appointments with medical experts, who are often complete strangers. They know nothing about who we are as unique individuals. The expert generally has little time to assess the particular qualities we possess. Yet we usually allow them, without any hesitation, to tell us what's wrong with us and how to fix it.

Most of the time, this health model actually works. We receive the necessary antibiotic, surgery, or cream that heals our body. But sometimes the cream only works for a short period of time. Or we are prescribed many different medications in search of the correct one, sometimes enduring side effects without attaining lasting health. Or the surgery doesn't work, and the now somewhat familiar practitioner recommends another one.

I believe that we are moving away from this old view of healing, and evolving a new model as we increasingly realize that each person is an integral part of a healing process. Though we will continue to rely on skillful practitioners to tell us our options, we'll also learn to trust that invaluable insights lead to the healthiest outcomes because they come from within. Where else could information about your health lie? Can it be locked away in someone else's awareness? Of course not.

Although we belong to one race and are anatomically similar, we each have a biochemical "fingerprint." Our internal chemistry differs from everyone else's because the complex organic matter that lives inside all of us is affected by emotions. Emotions, like everything in the universe, are made of pure energy. They form patterns in your body based on feelings you have expressed or repressed throughout your lifetime. Even if you are not aware of your feelings, they circulate within your body creating health, happiness, abundance, or the lack of these things.

If the energy arrangement in your body has created health problems, you can help change them by learning to feel your feelings—especially those you have chosen to ignore. Energy becomes stagnant when emotions do because energy moves in the body based on how we feel. Positive energy moving into the body prevents disease and helps the body heal if it becomes ill. When healthy energy moves in, it wakes stagnant energy from its lifeless slumber. Vital energy then pours in, helping tissue and organs function better and making all forms of medicine more effective, too.

As an intuitive healer, my job is to look, listen, and feel sensations that your biochemistry is expressing. Most people don't pay attention to what their being is sharing with them. Most hope they won't have to change at all, and that their health problems will simply vanish. The body in its infinite wisdom is asking you to change in some sort of mental, physical, emotional, or spiritual way to achieve wellness.

Modern medical discoveries still blow my mind away. It's incredible that new technology can help a twenty-five-week-old fetus survive outside of the womb. It's mind-boggling that cardiac surgeons no longer need to perform open-heart surgery to bypass occluded arteries. They now perform this with a lifesaving procedure known as MIDCAB (minimally invasive direct coronary artery bypass) in which several small incisions are made in the chest (sometimes with the help of a robot). The procedure reduces critical healing time and avoids the risk of infection. While modern medicine's advancements are truly remarkable, the expansion of energetic medicine is too.

Here's a good example of how conventional medicine contrasts with intuitive healing in recognizing and treating illness.

Recently, while treating a new client, I intuitively saw a small, pink, circular flashing light on the right side of her throat, an indicator to me that her thyroid was stressed and functioning at a lower-than-normal level. When I explained my findings, my client reported that she had routine blood work done the previous year, and her doctor said that her thyroid test came back low-normal. He said that he would retest her thyroid the following year, and if her thyroid numbers continued to decrease, he would prescribe a drug to counteract any potential health issues or symptoms.

I asked her thoughts about her doctor's recommendation. She said she'd asked him whether she could do something immediately instead of waiting for her numbers to potentially worsen and eventually taking prescription medication. Her doctor replied no.

Standard medical practice is to wait until symptoms arise or until test results indicate a medical condition. Then pharmacology or surgery is used to treat the problem. Energy medicine recognizes changes in the body before diagnosis and after. It works naturally with the body to help it re-experience its normal state of health, to avoid disease or heal if disease is present. To maintain a healthy immune system, it's critical to address potential disease and not wait for symptoms to arise or worsen.

Through our energy work, we could start the healing process on that day. First I detected a lack of energy at her thyroid gland and then re-established a positive flow of energy to the area through the fifth chakra (read more about the fifth chakra in chapter 6). I recommended easy exercises for her to do on her own to keep positive energy flowing to the area. I also recommended she schedule a follow-up visit with her physician or with a naturopathic physician, to clinically monitor her thyroid levels. We talked extensively about the emotional reasons why stagnant energy might have built up at her fifth chakra, potentially affecting her thyroid gland, and discussed what changes her body was asking her to make in her life. The insights I received from her body weren't foreign to her. Similar ideas had briefly come into her awareness, but she had not realized their wisdom until that day.

You may be wondering how it's possible to have awareness of your health without modern technology and to assist in your own healing or prevent disease. The answer lies within your feelings.

Feelings can be experienced as a physical sensation such as touch, warmth, tingling, or a gut feeling—a visceral reaction to something uncomfortable. Feelings can also be known as a state of consciousness resulting from emotions, sentiments, or desires. Emotions are multifaceted, resulting from internal biochemical and external environmental influences. All of them are direct messages from the deepest intelligence of your being.

When I work with clients, I'm constantly reading their emotions about their childhood and other prominent times in their life, which are related to their current situation. At the same time, I'm registering physical sensations that I feel. I know they play a key role in communicating to me how clients are experiencing the session and about how the energy is flowing in their body. They tell me whether they are relaxed;

cold or warm; which parts of our conversation create the highest awareness or "aha" moments for them; and which ideas I need to repeat or perhaps explain differently.

When the body is free of emotional stagnation, when we feel, understand, and express our real feelings, we become present and clear. Clarity allows each of us to become a multi-sensory being and better develop the three Clair's: clairvoyance, which means to see clearly; clairaudience, which means to hear clearly; and clairsentience, which means to feel clearly. Such clarity allows us to sense a limitless world beyond our ego-driven one, a world where we are free to receive information to heal and enjoy our lives in every capacity.

Assessing your amazing energy centers, located throughout the body, is one way you can evaluate the uniqueness that is alive inside you. It also allows you to gauge how your being feels during healthy times in your life, stressful phases, and instances when you face health challenges.

Throughout this book, you'll learn how to hear what your body is telling you about the connection between your health and emotions. By doing so, you'll find out how to prevent disease or heal from one that you might have. Intuitive healing is simple. It begins with you discovering your natural sensitivity to your body's powerful energy, which then opens you to a vastness inside you that is filled with loving energy.

2

First Chakra

Embracing Your First Family

A TALL, GRAY-HAIRED MAN WITH impatient blue eyes behind metal-rimmed glasses walks into my office for the first time. He beams as he enthusiastically stretches his hand out to greet me and introduces himself as Tom. His nervousness is palpable. He knows why he's here. I have no clue. As an intuitive healer, I prefer to read a new client's energy without any previous knowledge of his or her story. Not knowing the client's reason for seeing me lets me be emotionally neutral, which helps make my readings more accurate.

Despite Tom's friendly greeting, he looks stressed. His shoulders are up by his ears, and he taps his left foot on the beige carpet as if in a hurry. Even before I can ask him to remove his shoes and lie on the massage table, he anxiously blurts out, "How's my health?"

Surprised, I quickly scan his body from head to toe. My mind's eye observes plenty of motionless gray energy in his body. The darkest area is in his pelvis, but I find nothing overly alarming about his health. "There are some areas of concern, but overall you look fine to me," I say. Tom's shoulders ease, and he sighs in relief. "That's great! Because I have stage IV colon cancer, and my doctors advised me to get my things in order. I only have a few months to live."

"Really?" I answer, shocked. I scan his body repeatedly for evidence of terminal illness and death, but find none. As an experienced oncology nurse, I have seen many examples of stage IV colon cancer and know it means someone is close to the end of life.

Tom explains that he was diagnosed a little over five years ago, and that at the time his doctors estimated that he had only two years to live. He thinks that he outlived their prediction by doing the very things they said wouldn't help. He sought treatments from alternative medicine practitioners, took supplements, began eating a healthier diet, and even learned how to make fresh juices. He also traveled to the outskirts of Tijuana, Mexico, for experimental treatments, which he felt had made a big difference but were too costly for him to do on a regular basis.

I raise my eyebrows when he mentions traveling out of the country for treatment. I always worry about people who out of desperation travel abroad for a cure, potentially putting their health at risk and incurring great expense. But Tom seemed grateful for the care he had received.

I'm eager to work on Tom's energy system to understand why I don't think he's in danger of dying soon. As Tom lies down and rests his head on a pillow, I see a stream of multi-colored vital energy enter through his aura and begin pulsing. It illuminates my mind's eye and calms me. Tom relaxes, too, perhaps for the first time in years. I take a deep breath to clear my mind of worry. Telling a terminally ill man that he's fine is not how I typically start a session. Exhaling, I remind myself that my intuitions are meaningful for people. I might not know at first what they mean, but exploring them with my clients has helped many of them to heal. At this moment I'm particularly grateful for all the intuitive experiences I've had over the last six years since I left the hospital.

I tell Tom about two clients who I initially thought would survive their terminal illnesses, but who passed away. While telling him about these two misjudgments, I keep my third eye focused on his aura to see if the information alters his relaxation. The wavy, vibrant light show continues, which means that he remains relaxed. "I firmly believe you're not leaving this planet soon unless you want to," I tell Tom.

His blue eyes light up: "You're the first person to tell me I have a choice." He gently closes his eyes, and we resume our work.

When I begin working on Tom, I intuitively move my hands on top of his abdomen. I sense a wild storm of energy spinning out of control deep in his body, which I'll need to balance. My hands feel multiple folds of white areas of blockage, which are most likely cancer growths, throughout his abdominal area. In my mind's eye, I can see that the growths have attached to organs and tissues, and that they move when Tom moves. Digesting food has got to be painful.

I ask Tom if he has had any recent surgeries related to his cancer. "No, my doctors don't think surgery will be effective and that it would risk spreading the cancer." I let him know that the cancer has already spread beyond his abdomen. "That's right. The doctors told me that it's now in my lungs and liver." I ask him if he wants surgery, and he says, "Yes, my gut feeling is that it will be more helpful than harmful."

I nod my head in agreement: "Yes, your body is asking for it. Before my hands touched your abdomen, I heard this phrase repeating itself in my mind: 'Surgery would be best. Surgery would be best.'"

While I speak to Tom, it's as if a film is playing in my mind about an abdominal surgery with a colostomy procedure. Masses are removed from the abdomen, along with some of the intestines. While it plays, I explain to Tom that if he has the surgery, he might need a colostomy procedure. A colostomy procedure is when an artificial opening, called a stoma, is created through the abdominal wall from the colon, bypassing the diseased portion of the lower intestine. The procedure permits the passage of intestinal contents through the new opening. Postoperatively Tom would have to wear a bag over the stoma to collect intestinal waste.

"Would you be OK with that?"

"Yes, definitely!" he says. The film ends. I ask Tom if he's in any pain. He says no, that right now he's feeling peaceful. Just as he finishes speaking, my hands, which are still on his abdomen, feel as if they are being sucked into a dark, frenzied tornado, which forces my awareness deeper into his being. Energetically, I know I'm heading toward a mass of emotional pain buried deep within his first chakra. I also know that Tom has no idea it exists.

●　●　●

THE CHAKRA SYSTEM

The amazing chakra system plays an essential role in our physical, mental, emotional, and spiritual health. With more than three thousand small chakras and seven large primary chakras, your body is a highly organized energetic maze, responding to your every thought, feeling, and choice.

The chakras are cone shaped and located in the energy field of the human body. Their tips point deep into the body, while their bases lie just beneath the skin. Chakras spin.

They receive and transmit vital life-force energy into the body through this beautiful spinning motion.

The seven chakras are each a different primary color, and their bases are approximately two and a half inches in diameter. The primary chakras influence large anatomical areas of the body, and are connected to the emotional complexity of any one human life.

The smaller chakras are about the size of a nickel and influence smaller areas of the body, such as the joints, cartilage, muscles, subcutaneous tissue, and acupuncture points. Though they're small, their spinning is also powerful and beautiful. They glow a shimmering silver color while delivering surges of energy to specific locations in the body.

Understanding the role that emotions play in healing is essential to understanding the role of the chakras in healing. Feelings affect the choices we make, and our choices influence how and where energy moves in our body. Unfelt emotions build up in the body as stagnant energy, which can weaken a chakra's functions, reducing its ability to receive and transmit vital energy. Chakras that are deprived of energy can spin upside down or backward, become colorless, or develop holes in their structure. Fully feeling your emotions releases stagnant energy, allowing your energy system to maintain its health and vitality even during the most difficult times in life. Most people are afraid to feel, so they hide their emotions deep in the body, creating vast amounts of sluggish energy that ultimately can lead to disease. Unbalanced chakras are an indicator of potential disease in the body. Balanced chakras are vibrant in color and spin in a clockwise direction, signifying health.

Energy medicine recognizes the remarkable importance that emotions play in our health and well-being. Chakras

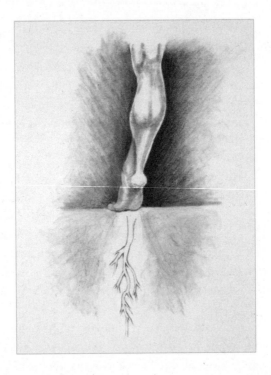

FIGURE 2. *The first chakra is often called the root chakra. Earth energy moves into the body through smaller chakras, present in the feet, and up through the root chakra.*

are the vehicles that steer health practitioners toward the emotional blocks that prevent healing and happiness.

First Chakra — Healing Your Roots

The first chakra is deep red and located in the pelvic floor. Its cone extends from the perineum to mid-thigh. As it rotates, it sends energy through the colon, large intestines, sciatic nerves, coccyx, bones, and the vessels that move blood throughout the lower half of your body.

The first chakra is connected to those emotions pertaining to our childhood or family of origin—our parents, siblings, grandparents, or other people who raised us. The size, shape, color, and function of your first chakra indicate how you felt growing up, and the belief system integrated into your conscious and subconscious mind.

The first step in healing your first chakra is to identify these core emotions: How did you feel about the homes and neighborhoods you lived in, or the schools you attended? Did you feel nurtured, loved, and safe in your family? If not, you may be ungrounded, tending to feel disconnected from the real world and making impulsive decisions.

* * *

As I merge into the gray, vertical funnel that is Tom's first chakra, I wonder why it's spinning so frantically. Where did all this emotional debris come from? I neither see nor feel any tragic childhood events. I force my gaze to bore through layers of dense suppressed feelings, but there are no horrible scenes. Mesmerized by the chaotic velocity, I silently stand by the massage table until I understand. To my surprise, Tom didn't need a tragic childhood to have a diseased body. Not feeling was all it took. Decades of unfelt emotions are locked inside Tom's body and spilling into his organs, creating an out-of-control disease.

Wanting to start a conversation about feelings and how to identify and experience them, I ask Tom, "So how was your childhood?" Given what I have just gleaned, his response is predictable: "Fine."

I doubt that Tom remembers much about his childhood. Feelings form memory. People recall little of their past if they didn't feel much then. When Tom first walked into my office, I had noticed that the mental field of his aura was about three feet larger in diameter than its more typical one-foot size. His oversized mental field means Tom's mind is always busy. Feeling *emotions* is a foreign experience for him.

"So how is your work going?" I ask. "Fine," he says again. I can tell that Tom works in a technical field from the way his mind is organized. In his frontal lobe I can see dark, linear lines partitioning compartments shaped like boxes. Just to be sure, I ask, "What do you do for work?"

"I'm an engineer."

"How is your family, Tom?"

"Great. They're all great."

I'm happy that he is more expressive about his wife and children, but I want to know more about his childhood.

"Are there other words besides 'fine' that you could use to describe your childhood or work?"

Tom takes a long pause before answering. "Hmm, I don't think so."

"Do you think the word 'fine' is a little too general? 'Fine' explains little and doesn't express emotion. Do you think that feeling your feelings is difficult for you?"

"No, Marie, I don't. Other than my health problems, my life is happy."

"What about your life makes you happy?"

"My kids are well, and I have a job."

"OK, great! What does happiness feel like?"

I can tell that my questions are stirring Tom's pent-up emotions. After each question an uncomfortable bee-like sting moves up my arms. Then I see fast-moving, frayed, red streaks moving through his aura—a signal to me that he is annoyed.

"I'm not sure what it feels like. I just know I'm happy," he says.

Not wanting to stop asking him about his emotions, I soften my voice, hoping the flaring red will dissipate.

"When was the last time you cried?"

"I don't know. I'm pretty sure I haven't cried in years unless we count when I received my diagnosis."

"OK, except for that, would you say decades?"

"Yes, decades."

"Do you think it's OK not to cry?"

"I haven't really thought about it."

Just then Tom's energy system alerts me to an "aha" that he is about to have. His entire aura becomes a beautiful white light. Thousands of cascading, brightly lit raindrops of energy pour into his body, falling from somewhere near the ceiling, energizing his consciousness. My questions about his childhood have woken the gray, stagnant energy from its heavy slumber. As the repressed energy moves, it speaks—or, rather, mumbles—like a tearful child unable to get its words out. I listen to the whimpering, stagnant energy rise from Tom's body in puffs of smoke. As the first smoky puff rises out and away from his body, I hear, "Children are meant to be seen, not heard."

The red, frayed streaks are gone. Tom is ready for more direct questioning.

"So what did you like about your childhood years?"

"I don't know, Marie."

"What did you not like about your childhood?"

"I don't know."

"Tom, are you seeing a theme here?"

"Yes. I think you're onto something. I'm missing a few feelings, and I'm realizing that I don't have many memories of my childhood."

"Tom, I think you have many bottled-up emotions lodged in the lower half of your body that are playing a large role in your health crisis."

"Are you recommending that I get to these feelings?" he asks.

"Yes."

"OK, so how do I do that?" Tom's request is sweet and sincere, as if he thinks feeling his emotions is a simple procedure, easily resolved by pushing a button.

"Let's begin by becoming aware of your current feelings. If you can be in the moment and feel your emotions, then those that are suppressed will emerge into your awareness and be released. Feeling emotions frees them from the body. When I look at your energy, Tom, I see a lot of energy going toward your brain thinking about work. Is that right?"

"Yes, I *do* have work on my mind. There is a lot of it, and I'm not sure if I can do it all. I want to take good care of my family."

"OK, we will get back to what to do about work, but right now I want to teach you how to be in the present moment through a technique called grounding."

· · ·

GROUNDING TO RECEIVE LIFE-SUSTAINING EARTH ENERGY

The word "grounding" in energy medicine means to receive healing, life-force energy from the earth into your body. Several small chakras are located on the bottom of both your feet, just below the surface of the skin. When a person is grounding, these small chakras release invisible energetic roots that grow through the feet and deep into the earth. Once the roots reach the core of the earth, they stop growing. The roots then burrow deep within the core and act like straws, receiving life-sustaining energy and pulling it into the first chakra. The first chakra uses earth energy to sustain the physical health of your human body. Grounding is the fundamental job of the first chakra.

Grounding to Help Our Children

Children diagnosed with attention deficit hyperactivity disorder (ADHD), attention deficit disorder (ADD), or who have difficulty sleeping can benefit from learning how to ground themselves. Their hyperactivity could be related to a poor diet, or a lack of exercise or a structured routine.

Children highly sensitive to the environment or certain foods tend to be more likely diagnosed with ADHD or ADD. These children can feel at peace if they eat mostly organic foods (without additives or food coloring) and spend more time outside and away from electrical devices, such as video games.

See one-minute grounding on page 23.

Grounding can be a difficult task for many people if they are not present in the moment. Most people think constantly, and thinking requires energy. Some people keep their minds

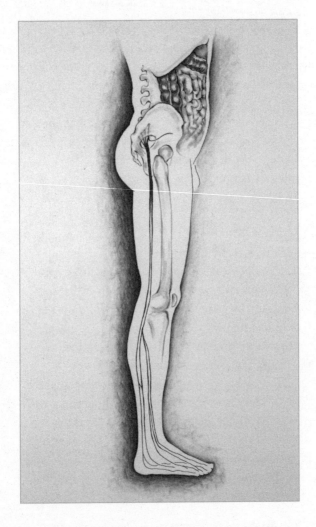

FIGURE 3. *The first chakra is the foundation of the entire ener-getic system. It governs the health of the colon, sciatic nerve, and many of the bones, including the pelvis, patella, tibia, and femur bones. It also governs DNA and is responsible for healthy blood and bone marrow.*

busy by processing a cascade of future possibilities, trying to solve problems that haven't yet materialized. Others constantly analyze the past, trying to change events that cannot be changed. And, of course, some people do both. Obsessive thoughts of the past and future waste precious energy intended for all the organs in your body, not just the brain. To be grounded also means to be present and aware of one's physical body.

* * *

"Tom," I say, "I would like you to physically feel some part of your body below your neck, to assist you in becoming present. Perhaps feel the socks on your feet, and then let the nerves in your feet feel the fabric, then the weight of the fabric and its warmth. Go ahead and move your awareness away from your thoughts and into your body. This exercise will help you get out of your head and into the present moment."

I know Tom will be able to do this exercise with little practice because he is relaxed. But like most people, he needs quite a bit of practice to let go and think less, to live in his body as opposed to his brain.

"Wow, I suddenly feel more at peace, as if my worries left my mind," Tom says. "My socks are really warm."

"This is what it feels like to be in the moment, Tom. Right now you're lying on a massage table, learning how to relax and heal. This moment has nothing to do with work. If you can get work out of your head, and be present for just a few moments at a time, you'll increase your level of awareness and allow your body to gather healing energy from the earth."

INCREASING AWARENESS

Ten quiet minutes pass. Tom is able to surrender to the bliss and freedom of not worrying. Then he opens his eyes. "What do you mean by increased awareness?"

"Great question. When you're thinking about things that have yet to occur or have already occurred, you're limiting your awareness of what's happening in the present. When you expand your consciousness of the present, you can make better-informed decisions."

I intuitively look at Tom's worries about work and supporting his family. When I look at his current reality, I see that it would be best for him to quit his job or at least work part-time. I see that financially he could do this because he has either downsized his home or paid off his mortgage. Tom has been responsible regarding his finances, and his wife works too, and their children are grown. The worries he has about supporting his family aren't based on facts. With his life-threatening illness, I can't think of a better time than right now to take an extended vacation from work or significantly reduce his hours.

I explain this to Tom, and he looks up at me, eyes wide open, as if he is a little shocked. "You're good."

Laughing, I say, "It's my job. But don't worry, I can't see how much money you have in the bank or any of your account numbers."

Knowing that Tom needs more convincing about working less, I try another tactic.

"If it were your wife who was ill, would you want her to work?"

Tom's eyes narrow as he says forcefully, "No, absolutely not!"

"Learning to receive is an important part of healing," I explain. "It's easier to make healthy choices for those we love than for ourselves. In the future, if you're not sure you're making the right choice, pretend that your situation is a problem for someone you love. The healthiest answer will follow."

It has been five years since Tom first walked into my office. He had surgery—which drastically reduced his pain—shortly after our first visit, and now has a colostomy bag. Tom also went from working as a full-time consultant to working part-time from his home. He comes to see me about every eighteen months when things get complicated. I help him navigate his life and medical choices since he still has cancer.

I saw Tom a few months ago following a lifesaving procedure that used laser technology to remove a tumor near his hip. The procedure was successful but caused a side effect called "foot-drop"—the inability to raise the front part of the foot. In Tom's case, this was because of nerve damage. With my hands, I energetically worked on his head to help stimulate nerves in his foot, and right away he felt sensations there.

That day Tom cried. As he sobbed, I realized it was one of the most beautiful things I have witnessed. Tom has been working on feeling his emotions throughout the past five years, and what strikes me most is that Tom is clear when he *isn't* feeling. He just needs to feel safe enough in order to feel. Thankfully, during his adventure into felt emotions, Tom could laugh and play with his family. I wish him many more years with them!

. . .

Earth Is Our Home

There are many reasons why we exist on Earth.
One of them is to learn how to live successfully
in this physical reality. Our miraculous planet
feels very female and nurturing to me. Just like a
mother who loves to give to her child, the earth
loves to give generously to those who live upon her.
I believe she also has emotions and a soul, and is
striving to learn how to balance her own unique
universe. As each of us learns to take responsibility
for our health, we also learn that we are responsible for the health of our planet. Human beings
cannot live well without earth energy, and the
earth cannot live well without the compassionate
care of human beings. With all of its beauty and its
problems, the earth is a unique place for souls to
evolve. We are in this together.

Exercises for the First Chakra

The following exercises are for the first chakra and all the
organs and systems it governs. They will help you to flow
vital life-force energy into your body from the earth. Take
the first chakra evaluation quiz first to help you determine
how grounded you are.

Quiz: First Chakra Evaluation

To find out how grounded you are, ask yourself the following questions:

	Yes	No
Do you like your body and the way you look?		
Are you comfortable receiving; do you allow others to give back to you?		
Do you feel safe in your family, community, and workplace?		
Do you feel safe living under the political rule of the country you live in?		
Do you feel that the earth is well and abundant?		
Do you spend time throughout your day feeling your emotions?		

If you answered yes to four or five of these questions, then you're very grounded to the earth and you are allowing your body to be fed by earth energy.

If you answered yes to three questions or fewer, it means you can improve your ability to receive earth energy into your body. Try the following exercises to improve how grounded into the earth you are.

One-Minute Grounding
My favorite exercise to help you ground can be done anywhere and in one minute. Its origin is based in Native American tradition.

1. Remove your shoes.
2. Stomp around your house or outdoors (outdoors is best) barefoot.
3. Make your hands into fists.
4. Punch your fists toward the earth as you stomp.
5. Say this phrase out loud while stomping: "I deserve to be here, and I live here in joy!"
6. Stomp for one minute, every day.

As you stomp around, the secondary chakras at the bottom of your feet will activate your energetic roots. You may notice a tingling sensation in your lower extremities or heaviness in your legs when you begin to pull earth energy into your body.

*

This exercise is great for children who have ADD, ADHD, or difficulty sleeping. They do not need to repeat the phrase while stomping. For children with insomnia, this exercise is best done right before bed. See page 17 for more information.

Grounding through Visualization

Creative visualization is another way to charge your energy so you'll be more grounded to the earth. This exercise takes ten minutes.

1. Sit in a comfortable chair.
2. Place your feet flat on the floor.
3. Rest your hands on your lap with the palms facing up.
4. Close your eyes and take several deep breaths.
5. Imagine breathing in tranquil energy and breathing out stress and anxiety.
6. Practice breathing calmly for about five minutes, or until you feel relaxed.
7. Bring your attention to the bottom of your feet, and then visualize several small chakras just beneath the skin. (Remember, chakras look like cones that point deep into the body, while their wider base is just beneath the skin.)
8. Visualize the small chakras spinning in your feet.

9. Do your best to *feel,* or sense, the chakras spinning in your feet.
10. Once you feel connected to your feet, creatively visualize roots growing out of the cones.
11. Visualize the roots growing out of your feet.
12. Visualize the roots growing into the floor under your chair.
13. Visualize the roots growing through the foundation of the building you're in and into the earth.
14. Creatively visualize your roots growing thousands of miles into the earth, through mountains and oceans, until they reach the core of the earth.
15. Allow your roots to spread out horizontally while remaining rooted to the core of the earth.
16. Imagine your roots transforming from growing downward to receiving.
17. Begin drawing up earth energy into your roots.
18. Continue to draw up earth energy through thousands of miles of roots and into your body.

3

Second Chakra

Becoming Passionate

"I THOUGHT I COULD STOP wanting a baby, but I can't," Dauri says. A thirty-nine-year-old schoolteacher, she has undergone four artificial insemination treatments since our first session. All of them failed. Last week, before her second session with me, her doctor canceled the fifth treatment minutes before it was scheduled. He told Dauri that her uterus wasn't responding to the hormone therapy, making it impossible for the treatment to work.

I take a break from her sadness and focus my gaze on my hands to gather insight. They rest on Dauri's striped shirt, just below her belly button. I feel physically detached from them, yet my emotions are racing with Dauri's feelings of disappointment and grief. Her anxiety fills her aura and spills into mine, screaming, "There may never be a baby in my belly!"

Even though she is heartbroken, the fact that Dauri is feeling emotions at all is a vast improvement over her first visit. When I met her six months ago, I was instantly curious about her second chakra which sits in the lower abdomen. While she sat several feet away from me in a creamy leather chair in my waiting room, dark gray bursts of energy pulsed from her lower abdomen, aimed at their target—me—like a homing device. Her second chakra was calling out to me, hoping I could help. I didn't yet know what the problem was when we first met. When I finally touched her lower abdomen, I perceived some sort of rigid container in her pelvis. I merged with it and landed in a pile of anger. The anger was blatantly obvious, making the walls of my office energetically throb like mad drums. How could I have missed this fury? It was so strong that I certainly didn't need to touch her to discover it. Then I realized that the energetic container had prevented me from sensing it. Dauri, like many women, had repressed her anger. Her rage was completely filling her pelvic cavity. My awareness drifted from the container to an image of a woman in the center of Dauri's abdomen that I intuited was her mother.

• • •

THE JUICY CHAKRA

The second chakra responds to all of your wild, wonderful, and difficult emotions: your personal feelings about yourself and your passions—for your career, finances, creativity, and relationships (both friendships and partnerships). This is why I call the second chakra the juicy chakra. Much of what we desire and worry about in life is directly connected to the second chakra. Believe it or not, most people feel very little passion—which I would define as a deep desire to do something or be a part of something that brings them inspiration, happiness, or just plain fun.

Repressed anger and guilt are the two main emotions that block passion in the second chakra. Typically, women repress anger and men repress guilt. Both types of repression can create health problems in the lower back, kidneys, adrenal glands, appendix, bladder, and reproductive organs and their glands. This is why the second chakra is the emotional response center.

The second chakra is bright orange and is located in the lower abdomen, just below the belly button. As it rotates, it sends energy through the reproductive organs, kidneys, adrenal glands, bladder, appendix, and lower back. Unlike the first and seventh chakras, chakras two through six have two cones (mates), one positioned at the front of the body and one at the back. (The first and seventh chakras are considered mates in their own respect.) The mates are arranged in a vertical column along the spine. The second chakra's mate is located in the lumbar area of the spine.

The chakra cones located along your back represent your will. "Will" refers to our conscious and sometimes subconscious action, thought, intent, or purpose. We can influence our lives by exerting our will, or we can get out of the way and let the will of the Divine flow into our lives, aligning us with our highest good. When we exert our will to control others or hold ourselves back, we do so out of fear. We might think we are afraid of illness, poverty, loneliness, or crime, but what we fear most is our power—the infinite power we all possess. This power is radically different than the power that governments, militaries, and banking institutions impose on the world. This unlimited power is compassionate and drenched with infinite love for all that exists in the universe.

Exercise for Improving Back Health

Poor back health is related to forcefully willing something to happen. To create healthy flowing energy in the spine, try repeating this mantra a few times a day for several minutes: *I surrender, I surrender, I surrender . . .* Many of my clients have found relief from back pain and other spinal health concerns by saying this simple phrase.

• • •

FEELING EMOTIONS

During her first session, Dauri had no idea that she was holding repressed anger in her pelvis. I told her about it and gave her exercises to help release it. I hoped the container would eventually leave her body, signaling her desire to feel emotions in the moment rather than storing them in her body. I worried that this would be difficult for Dauri because she, like about 15 percent of my clients, can't feel energy moving in her body. This makes it difficult to recognize stagnant energy or feel a need to do the energetic exercises I prescribe.

Historically, Dauri had experienced many of the common symptoms of repressed anger in the pelvis, including tumors in her uterus and other female ailments such as painful menses. A few years before we met, she had surgery to remove uterine fibroids. She had no idea that her reproductive health issues would resurface when she and her partner, Kim, decided to have a baby.

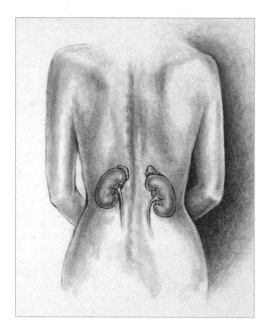

FIGURE 4. *The back mate of the second chakra is near the kidneys, which sit just below the adrenal glands. These organs function well when we have happiness in our lives.*

Kim, nine years younger than Dauri, is a tall, athletic massage therapist in private practice. Dauri and Kim met in the Pacific Northwest, but they both grew up in the Deep South. Kim never had the desire to carry a child, and their physician warned them that Dauri could face infertility, pre-term labor, and increased risk of giving birth to a child with birth defects because she was in her late childbearing years. Weighing this information, the couple decided that adoption was the best option.

During their initial interview at the state adoption agency, the social worker surprised Dauri and Kim by saying, "I think you should try having your own child." Dauri swears she never told the social worker about her desire to conceive. They thought the social worker's words were a sign.

Today, Dauri is experiencing grief. Even though it's painful to feel, I'm delighted that she is on the right track. Repressed anger can act like a blanket, further suppressing other emotions such as sorrow and grief—emotions that are generally more challenging to face. When anger lifts from the body, these challenging emotions follow.

Staring into her pelvic cavity, I see her mother in the middle of Dauri's reproductive organs, just as I had during our first appointment. To be sure of the woman's identity, as I don't always remember details from previous sessions, I describe her.

"Dauri, there is a woman in your second chakra, and I think it's your mom. Is your mom about five foot three, of medium weight, with lovely blue eyes and soft gray-blond hair?"

"Yes."

Immediately after Dauri speaks, I hear a loud boom in my head, as if thunder is roaring in the sky. The loud rumble represents the difficulty of this mother-daughter relationship, which is most likely one of the primary reasons Dauri is having trouble conceiving.

"Dauri, I know you're feeling sad right now, but I want you to know that the energy exercise you have been practicing since our first session is paying off."

Dauri smiles faintly, a measure of hope in her face. "Even though I'm devastated about the failed inseminations," she says, "I reevaluated my desire to get pregnant during a long conversation with Kim. We also visited our naturopath, who had been helping me balance my hormones, and we decided to try again by thinking positively and doing energy work."

"Great," I say. "I'm more than happy to help with energy work, and help you and Kim think and feel positively about your future family. The first thing we need to do is release as much anger as we can that is stored in your pelvic cavity. You are unconsciously blocking your ability to get pregnant because you're still angry at your mother and afraid you will parent a child the way your mom parented you."

"Yes, that feels true. I know I'm still mad at her, yet afraid I'll be like her."

When I ask Dauri about the kind of relationship she has with her mother, she bursts out crying and says she tries hard not to think about it. I explain that trying not to think about it is in fact repressing her anger. If we work together to release it, I tell her, then her reproductive organs will have a chance to heal.

Dauri takes a deep breath and sighs, freeing a small tear from her right eye. "I'm feeling a lot of anger because she doesn't understand me and I don't get that. I'm her daughter and a good person, but I'm not like her—she's a true Southern woman, and I'm not. I wonder at times, even if I were more like her, would we get along better?"

"Good, these are the feelings that you need to feel and release."

I dig a little deeper and discover that the divide between mother and daughter has been there for Dauri's whole life. Her mother always wanted Dauri to do things her way, which suggests that she may have had control issues.

"I know this is hard, Dauri, but we all need to learn that we have free will. Knowing that you might have some of your mother's traits makes you more aware of yours, giving you an opportunity to make choices that are different than hers. Have you thought that perhaps you are a teacher for your mother regarding her control issues?"

The vibration of the word *teacher* echoes through my office and begins shifting some of Dauri's repressed anger closer to the surface of her lower abdomen, oozing some of it out of her body, like faint dull smoke.

Dauri looks perplexed. She opens her eyes and meets mine. "No," she says. "What do you mean by that?"

"Well, Dauri, I believe we are here on Earth to experience being human for many reasons. The main reason is to gain awareness so that we may change our perceptions and raise our consciousness. Children, because they are so fresh from creation, are our best teachers and provide many opportunities for growth to their parents. Even the most dysfunctional families have vast opportunities for growth."

Shocked, Dauri squeezes her eyebrows together. "Are you saying that the difficulty I have with my mother serves a purpose?"

"Yes, you and I know that the two of you get along better when she accepts you as you are, giving her opportunities to learn how not to control. And your dislike of her influential nature allows you to learn to be different, too. Ultimately we are all teachers for one another."

Our conversation helps Dauri reach a peaceful place inside herself. Warm energy spreads a smile across my face, adding to the genuine love now pervading both of our auras. Profound truth vibrates, filling the room and Dauri's energy system with love, allowing her to glimpse her personal lessons. Her body lets me know that she is feeling amazing, so I ask her what she is sensing.

"It's incredible—my whole body is tingling. I feel so much love in my chest. I don't want this feeling to go away."

I'm quiet for several minutes, wanting to let Dauri feel this natural state of being as long as possible. After a while I say, "Dauri, can you sense a lesson you may want to learn about relating to your mother?"

"Yes! I can actually see it. I'm recalling parts of my childhood and feeling lucky. Despite what felt like my mother judging me, I see that she has given me the green light to be an independent woman. I can feel how much she loves me, and at this moment I know our child will bring Kim's family and mine closer together."

"Is there something in particular that you see, Dauri?"

"Yes, I'm three years old, swinging in a park that I had completely forgotten about. It's spring, and there are many dandelions all over the grass. I remember really liking the happy yellow flowers. My mom is pushing me, and I keep asking her to push me higher. She's smiling and telling me how brave I am as she pushes me higher and higher. It's almost like I can feel her thoughts. She's checking my safety. Is my butt snug in the seat? If I were to fall off, what would I hit? At the same time, she doesn't want me to be afraid. She wants me to feel free."

"Congratulations, Dauri, you're experiencing joy. You now have a choice. You can feel the old feelings about your relationship with your mom, or you can choose your new feelings discovered in this moment."

* * *

KUNDALINI ENERGY

Everything in life has a passionate feeling that radiates as color, light, smell, texture, sound, and taste with a kind of orgasmic energy. When we permit our senses to perceive our universe as vibrant, we activate pleasure and stimulate dormant energy lying in the pelvic cavity. This energy is called Kundalini.

Kundalini energy emerges from the pelvis at the front cone of the second chakra. When released from its slumber, it stimulates the pelvic cavity and arouses joy. It then moves into the back of the second chakra and begins an upward movement through the spine. Moving from vertebra to vertebra, it circulates in an electric blue, figure-eight pattern until it reaches the occipital ridge at the back of the head. Kundalini energy then enters the brain and fuels the pituitary, pineal, and hypothalamus glands. Arousing these glands awakens the inner knowledge and insight present in each human being. Insight allows us to become aware of the beauty present in all things.

• • •

"Dauri, I'm so impressed with the hard work you did today and all the work you did in between sessions. I feel confident that you will have a new being in your life to learn from."

Dauri smiles teary-eyed and says, "I hope so."

Before Dauri leaves my office, I ask her to ask Kim to consider coming in for a session because she is an equal participant in fulfilling the couple's desires.

The following week Kim visits. She and I had met many years before at a wellness event. Comfortable with one another, we get to the subject matter right away.

"Marie, I just don't know about this whole baby thing," she tells me. "The procedures are expensive, and none of them have worked. I love Dauri and want a baby too, but it feels like a baby will complicate our lives."

Kim sits nervously in a chair, swaying her knees gently from side to side. I am not sure if she wants to get on the massage table for her session or just talk from where she sits. She still wears several layers of outdoor clothing. Her aura is drab and fuzzy, and her second chakra retracts deep within her pelvis, letting me know that she isn't telling the whole story—not because she's lying, but because she's as yet unaware of it.

"You're right, babies are a lot of work, but you already know this. What else do you think is complicated about parenting a child?" I ask, tapping the table to let her know I'm ready for her. Kim purses her lips with a look of concern, stands, and begins taking off her jackets.

"I guess what's most challenging for me is that everyone will know for sure that Dauri and I are a gay couple," Kim says as she reclines on the table.

"Is that a problem?"

"Technically, no. I don't hide the fact that I'm gay, and my parents are great about my lifestyle. But if we have a child, then all the people outside of our family and friends will know for sure that I'm gay."

"Is that a problem?"

"Yes, I think it is for me." Kim's cheeks flush a light shade of crimson.

I lay both of my hands on Kim's abdomen and move comforting light into the lower area to help her feel at ease with her embarrassment. The light invites her second chakra to move; it floats up to my hands, briefly resuming a normal position, then floats away. Her chakra repeats this movement many times, like a wave, winking at me.

"Your feelings are normal, Kim. No one wants to be stared at or have their lifestyle questioned at work or by strangers you run into at the grocery store. Right now, feeling your embarrassment is helping you heal."

"I hate the feeling. It's so uncomfortable."

"I know. Everyone does. But not feeling your emotions keeps them in the body and limits your awareness. I bet you haven't been able to feel positive about having a child with Dauri."

"You're right. It's been really hard. I want to, but I can't seem to feel happy about having a baby."

"No wonder, Kim. You're afraid to let people outside of your support circle of friends and family know who you are, and you're embarrassed about feeling that. With all that going on, who could be happy?"

Kim's breath slows, transitioning to deep-belly breathing. Tears roll down her cheeks as she relinquishes the shame, flooding the room with the energetic vapors of old, long-repressed feelings. I smile radiantly, silently thanking her for having the courage to stay present through the sting of her feelings.

After a few moments I break the silence. "Kim, let's imagine that your fears are just that, fears, and that something very different is most likely to happen when you and Dauri create an extension to your family. Let's imagine that you and Dauri have a child and you're out in public, shopping, working, or returning home from work. People stop to admire and coo at the baby. No one asks about your relationship status or if the child has two mothers. Seeing a child's face is generally a welcome invitation to fuss over them and feel joy for a new life."

The lines of tension on Kim's face dissolve into a chuckle. "I never thought of it that way, but you're right—most people love babies."

"Kim, the future has yet to happen, and what you focus on draws it toward you. Concentrating on feeling happier

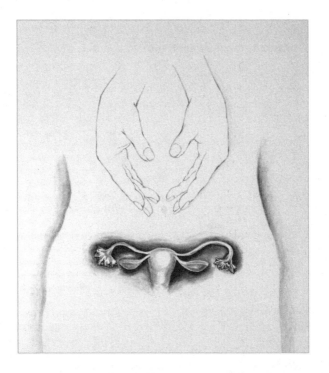

FIGURE 5. *The second chakra governs the health of the reproductive organs, including the uterus, ovaries, and fallopian tubes. The hands in this drawing represent Kim and Dauri coming together to creatively manifest their family.*

attracts your desired outcomes to you. Each moment you have a choice to feel joy or not."

"Why is this so hard to practice?"

"Our world is plagued with negative thinking. Most people have a hard time with change and will stick with what's familiar, even if it's not giving them what they truly want. Let's create an image and generate feelings that will allow you to focus on what you want. Imagine that you and Dauri have created the family of your dreams and you're all very joyful. How would that feel if what you want is already here, and there is no need to worry or strenuously think to solve these difficult problems?"

"That would feel great."

"Wonderful. When creating anything, feeling how the end result would feel is all that's necessary. Focusing on the small details of how to get there creates worry. Worrying pushes your desires away and creates more worry. Get clear on what it would feel like to have a child in your life, then feel that for a few moments every day. Then the baby will come in the most breathtaking way possible."

"Really, that's it? Don't I need to consider how to raise money for the next insemination, or when Dauri should do another procedure?"

"No."

"Marie, that's the complete opposite of how I usually think."

"I know, Kim. When things work out best, they work out magically—in ways no one could have imagined. When you let go of the planning and the over-analysis of how things should be, you engage your creativity and learn to trust that amazing things will come your way."

After Kim's visit, she and Dauri practiced feeling positive emotions on a daily basis, imagining welcoming a baby into their family. After a short time, they felt inspired to clean out the spare bedroom to make space for a baby. They both imagined the baby's room freshly painted with cheerful colors and filled with all the necessary clothing, toys, crib, and other items. Both commented later that the clearing birthed a new idea to help resolve their dilemma.

Even though Kim did not want to carry a baby in her body, she realized that she would not be opposed to contributing her eggs. Kim's eggs were younger than Dauri's and therefore more viable. Contributing her eggs would also allow her to be directly involved in the pregnancy. Dauri was ecstatic.

Just before the scheduled insemination, Dauri learned that her great-aunt had passed away. She left Dauri an unexpected inheritance she had stowed away in shoeboxes beneath her bed. The inheritance paid for the procedure.

Dauri became pregnant on the first insemination with Kim's eggs. A few weeks later they discovered that Dauri was expecting twins. Dauri gave birth to a healthy boy and girl, who are now six years old. They both look just like Kim.

• • •

Exercises for the Second Chakra
The following exercises are for the second chakra and all the organs and systems it governs. They will help you to flow vital life-force energy into your body to support your emotions and create a happy and fulfilling life.

Bring Joy into Your Life
I know it's hard to imagine that something as simple as a thought can lead to a feeling, and that that feeling can create outcomes. The reason it's true is because thoughts are made of energy, just like everything in the universe. If we learn to focus positively on authentic desires and become willing to rethink our fears, anything is possible.

Following are six questions you can ask yourself in order to gauge the amount of passion you currently have in your life. Before answering, take a few moments to center yourself, so that you can respond honestly to the questions from a deep place within your being.

Step 1: Center Yourself

The term *center* means to remove busy activity from your mind, such as worries or lists of daily duties that disconnect you from the present moment. Here are two centering exercises to choose from:

- Sit in a quiet place with your hands in your lap, palms turned up toward the ceiling. Close your eyes, and inhale and exhale slow, deep breaths for several minutes until you notice that your mental chatter has quieted.
- Stand with your legs shoulder-width apart, with your knees slightly bent. Place your hands near your belly button, palms facing your body, with your elbows also bent. Begin sweeping your hands up along your body toward your chest. When your hands reach your chest, move them out and away from your body, and then down toward your abdomen. When your hands are moving up toward your chest, inhale, and when they are moving out and away from your body, exhale. Continue this exercise until you reach mental relaxation.

Step 2: Rate Your Joy

After you feel centered, rate your joy concerning your home, job, money, friends, family, partner, and creativity by using the corresponding number for the five statements provided. Examples of joy are feeling ecstatic, fabulous, better than imagined, or grateful.

1	I dislike it.
2	I don't have an opinion. (If other people feel happy, then it's OK with me).
3	It's OK.
4	I'm happy with it.
5	I feel joyful about it.

Your home _____
Your job _____
Your relationship with money _____
Your friends _____
Your relationship with your children and/or
     other family members _____
Your relationship with your partner _____
Your relationship with creativity _____

After you finish rating your joy, add up the number of points from each answer. Here's what the different totals mean about your capacity to feel joy in your life right now.

Points	Joyfulness
6–12	You have yet to figure out what joy feels like. It can be difficult to create a joyful life when joy is an unknown feeling. Focus on a time in your life when you were happy. Use the memory of that feeling as a measuring tool. In the future, when making a choice, choose only those things that remind you of the happy time in your life. Do your best to walk away when the feeling is not there. Use this exercise often, so that you may experience happiness more often and realize you are valuable and deserve joy! Then move on to the next exercise.

Points	Joyfulness
13–18	You have some idea what happiness feels like, but you're most likely concerned with the happiness of another person rather than your own. Feeling happiness for others is a temporary fix. No matter how hard we try, we can't control the feelings of others. True happiness is an individual experience. Getting to know your desires is what allows a person to feel happy. Ask yourself: what food, music, or activity is my favorite? Getting to know your likes and dislikes and choosing the ones *you* like best leads to happiness. And happiness is on the road to joy! When you can recognize happiness independent of others, move on to the next exercise.
19–24	You definitely know what happiness feels like, and sometimes joy sneaks up and surprises you! You are most likely wondering how to keep that elusive feeling that tingles on the inside. Many times you allow yourself only a small amount of joy, wondering if you're being selfish or perhaps worried that if you feel too much, something bad will happen. Remember, living a joyful life is normal. When the feeling arrives, hold on to it as long as you can. Your body will appreciate the positive flow of energy! When you can hold on to a joyful feeling most of the day, move on to the next exercise.

Points	Joyfulness
25–30	You're doing it—you're creating a joyful life! You may at times feel like an outsider, as most humans feel very little joy. But your dedication to living a wonderful life subconsciously helps others to do the same. You most likely have discovered that being joyful is an experience, one that is created by filtering out choices—choosing the happiest and ignoring the runners-up. Thank you for choosing you! Please continue your great joy!

One-Minute Balancing

Have little time? Then try this easy, one-minute exercise to release stagnant energy from the pelvis and free up your creativity.

Standing with your feet shoulder-width apart, begin rotating your hips first clockwise, then counterclockwise for one minute. When you rotate your hips to the right you are activating masculine energy. Male energy runs on the right-hand side of the body. When you rotate your hips to the left you are activating female energy, which runs on the left-hand side of the body. This exercise will balance your male and female energies through your emotional response center.

•

Children balance their male and female energies by feeling their surroundings with their senses. Plants, trees, air, bikes, and even jungle gyms are made of energy and pulsate a feeling that children can pick up. We are all sensitive beings, but children are even more so. When putting on their tennis shoes, ask them to feel their shoelaces with their fingers and experience the dance their fingers create when making the knot. As humans become socialized, we tend to lose our innate ability to recognize subtle sensations. When children engage their senses with the world around them, they feel happier and more hopeful about life.

Releasing Anger

For some people, releasing anger happens when least expected and generally requires an apology. Others choose to avoid the whole sordid experience of anger and steer clear of conflict. Anger, however, is a normal emotion. When expressed safely, it becomes a channel for clearing the body of stagnant energy.

1. Find a private room and lie on the floor.
2. Throw a temper tantrum from one to five minutes. Kick, scream, and pound your fists into the floor.

It's not necessary to feel angry to practice this exercise. In fact, most people to whom I give this exercise tell me they aren't angry. Their anger is so repressed that they have no awareness of it.

Releasing Guilt

Releasing guilt is important because we're always doing the best we can. When we know better, we do better.

1. Lie on your back for five to ten minutes.
2. Place your dominant hand gently on your lower abdomen, just below your belly button.

3. Close your eyes and repeat, either out loud or
   silently in your mind, the following mantra: *I have
   always done the very best I could, in every situation
   of my life, with what I knew at the time.*

This exercise works wonders in helping men heal from
poor prostate gland health.

— 4 —

Third Chakra

Learning to Love Yourself

A MAN WITH A CONTAGIOUS smile greets me with a cry of "Marie!" as I enter the hallway between my office and the bathroom. Either he has arrived a little early, or I'm running late. I must know him, I think, embarrassed that I'm drawing a blank; I rarely remember the names or faces of my clients. To avoid disappointing him, I mentally run through a list of male names: Jim, Mike, Randy, John, Bill, Frank. None matches this face.

Many years ago I realized that not remembering my clients protects both me and them. It prevents me from worrying about them as they work to heal themselves. It allows me to be fully in the present, in grace, with each client, and gives a peaceful end to my day.

I stand eye to eye with my client and notice that he's already taken off his shoes in preparation for our session. "Hi," I say with a wide smile, hoping he will blurt out his name while I shake his hand. The handshake grows a little intense. As if he knows my inner dilemma, he says, "We have never met, but my wife is in your mentoring program, and I listen to your radio show all the time. I'm Mark."

"Oh, Mark, it's so nice to meet you!" Our hands fall away from the lively shake. Instantly I remember Mary, one of my mentoring students, telling me last week that her husband had made an appointment with me. The mentoring program is a yearlong curriculum for those who work in the field of energy medicine and wish to expand their knowledge and skill base. It's also for people who have intuitive skills and abilities to move energy and would like to learn more and perhaps create a private practice.

"Your wife is a lovely person. I truly enjoy her presence in the mentoring program."

I breathe an inner sigh of relief now that I know who this smiling, shoeless man is. I'm reminded once again that my radio show brings people close to me, even though I have never met them.

Moments later, Mark is lying on his back on the massage table; his lightly thinning dark hair rests on the pillow and his big blue eyes look straight up at me. I'm standing on his left side with my hands energetically deep within his solar plexus, the third chakra. A forceful tug has drawn my hands there, making it difficult to move them anywhere else on his body. My mind alerted me to the area as soon as Mark lay down. The area looks like a black crater instead of a chakra. Lonely and empty, the hole's depth is difficult to measure, as is the personal pain he is trying to hide. As I watch the crater, Mark's personality reveals itself to me.

I can see that his energy is an equal mix of feminine and masculine—though I'm not sure if he would be comfortable knowing that. He is kind, honest, and a real worrier. I'm not sure he would want to hear about that either, but it will be a large part of our conversation today. Mark is also intuitive and more consciously aware of himself and life than the average person. Surprisingly, I see the numeral two. I don't know what its significance is, but it keeps coming into view no matter where I look into his energy system. More important than figuring that out now, though, I need to find out why his digestive system is a wreck.

"Mark, how is your digestion these days?"

"Well, that's the main reason I'm here. Ten years ago I had digestive problems, but even after giving me many tests, my doctor couldn't diagnose the problem. So I stopped taking the medication he prescribed that wasn't working. I made adjustments to my lifestyle, and the pain went away and stayed away until recently. My new doctor wants to do more testing because neither the holistic nor the Western medicine is working. My pain is pretty high and conflicts with my ability to work and enjoy my family. I feel I need to change my lifestyle instead of taking more tests. I was hoping you could help me figure out what those changes might be."

When Mark speaks of his pain, I can clearly see a hospital pain chart numbered one through ten. Doctors and nurses use such charts to help patients identify their pain level. When their pain reaches a four or five, it helps them ask for pain medication to avoid intractable pain. The number nine is highlighted in the chart in my mind. This means Mark is feeling a significant amount of pain. I wish he had taken a few more medical tests.

Mark tells me that he has been on antidepressants for years. They have been effective, but he now worries that if the digestive pain doesn't go away, it could escalate his depression.

"What changes did you make ten years ago?"

"Well, I was a teacher then, and I quit teaching."

"So the pain went away when you stopped teaching?"

"Yes."

"What do you do now?"

"I'm a therapist."

"What about teaching do you think led to the digestive problems?"

"I worried about my students."

"In what way?"

"I worried about their lives at home."

As Mark speaks, I can see the third eye in his forehead, which alerts the conscious mind to what it perceives. The third eye widens and blinks, confirming to me that he has an intuitive nature. Staring into the eye, I see an image of an adolescent boy. A boy Mark taught. A boy Mark had accurately intuited as having serious problems at home. A boy he apparently was unable to help.

"Are you worrying about one of your former students now?"

"Yes," Mark says, opening his eyes to look at me. "You can see that?"

I smile at him. He knows about my abilities, and I feel no other reply is necessary. Mark grins too, then closes his eyes again.

Born and raised in Boston, Mark taught English to eighth- and tenth-grade students in the late 1980s and early '90s. Some kids had it rough; they came from broken homes and had difficulty with their peers. There wasn't a lot he could do to help them in a one-hour class.

"Do you worry about your patients?"

"Sure, but it's never bothered me before. If I didn't worry about them, they would wonder whether I was compassionate or cared about the concerns that brought them to my office."

I can feel Mark beginning to worry; the sensation reminds me of the many times I have worried about my children. The numeral two appears again in his energy, followed by a familiar feeling, which I have learned to trust over time, telling me that the numeral is a reference to years.

"What has changed in your life over the past two years?"

"I now have a child."

"Yes, of course, congratulations. How old is she?" I remembered that Mark's wife, Mary, had been contemplating having another child, but had said Mark was unsure about it.

"She's almost two," he says.

"Mark, have you noticed that my hand has not moved from your solar plexus area? Your third chakra literally doesn't want me to leave."

"Yes, I can feel it there. Your hand feels hot."

"There is a substantial amount of motionless energy in your solar plexus. When a chakra generates heat when I place my hands on it, it means that large amounts of stagnant energy are present. My hands literally get busy and infuse the area with light. Eventually the increased vital force creates pressure—just like atmospheric pressure in the sky before it rains. This pressure causes the less-vital energy—usually trapped, unfelt emotions—to release and move out of the body."

■ ■ ■

THE THIRD CHAKRA—A HEALTHY IMMUNE SYSTEM

The third chakra is located in the solar plexus, between the opening of our rib cage. Anatomically, it oversees the gall bladder, spleen, stomach, liver, pancreas, and small intestine. Emotionally, the third chakra is about self-love. This bright-yellow chakra has another responsibility—it governs your immune system, because in addition to the mentioned organs, it directs energy to the glands in your body (adrenal, ovaries, testes, prostate, thyroid, pineal, hypothalamus, and

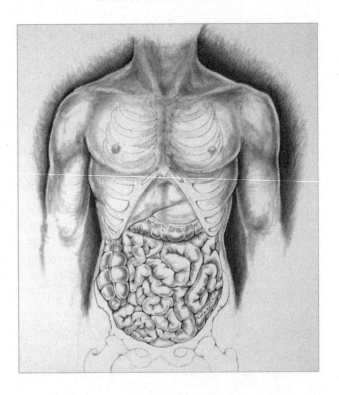

FIGURE 6. *Eighty percent of your immune system's functions lie in your small intestines, which are shown here along with a partial view of the liver and stomach.*

pituitary; the pancreas is considered both a gland and an organ). Glands release hormones into the body. Hormones act as tiny messengers, regulating the function of your organs, and so contribute in a significant way to the health of your immune system.

Surprisingly, 80 percent of your immune system's functions are located in your thirty-foot long intestinal tract. A healthy intestinal tract is necessary for proper absorption of nutrients and for releasing harmful waste products. If it functions poorly, toxins (unhealthy substances such as processed foods, alcohol, and environmental pollutants) build up on the intestinal wall, where they are absorbed into the body.

Thoughts and feelings about ourselves, along with environmental toxins, play a role in the health of our immune system. Kind and loving thoughts and feelings vastly improve the immune system. When we are disappointed in ourselves, or react emotionally to the negative things that others say to us, we weaken our immune systems and hold onto toxins. To some degree or another, all of us need to work on self-love.

Our awareness of autoimmune disorders is increasing, and they are difficult to diagnose and treat because most are identified through a process of elimination, which means you must take test after test. Once a diagnosis is determined, conventional medicine uses treatments to repress the immune system further in order to reduce symptoms.

Holistic medicine looks at the whole person, not just test results and symptoms. When we become ill, our body is trying to tell us something. Illness is meant to draw our attention inward. I can just hear Mark's third chakra saying, "Hey you, over here. Yeah, you. I love you, man. I am so proud of you, and everything you think you did wrong is right. Thank you for being you."

What medical science is beginning to understand is that a breakdown of the immune system is often a precursor of disease. When I treat a client with a disease, I work deeply with the immune system, and for me that means the third chakra.

· · ·

Thus far the energy treatment is already starting to create change in Mark's body. I can see what looks like grey smoke rising in a plume at rapid speed from Mark's third chakra. There is no change in his facial expression, but I feel a calming energy spread through his body.

"How are you feeling, Mark?"

Mark takes a few moments to respond. "Odd . . . I can feel my body and mind let go. I think I'm relaxing!"

"Wonderful. How is the pain in your digestive system?"

"Better," he says, surprised.

"Mark, you have an amazing ability to understand how others feel; this is one of the reasons why you are so good at your work. However, I think you are somewhat unaware of your own emotions. In fact, I think you feel your clients' and other people's emotions so well that you frequently adopt them as your own."

"Hmm. I would have to think about that," he says.

"Instead of thinking up a response, could you feel one? Empathic people, like yourself, are naturally intuitive and are generally drawn to careers that allow them to help others. It's easy for you to feel for another, but maybe not for yourself."

"Marie, I hear you and understand intellectually what you're asking me to do, but I have no idea how to go about it."

"Wonderful!"

Mark chuckles. "Are you always this positive?"

"The fact that you can't do what I'm asking means we are on the right track. Mark, I think your empathy becomes much harder to balance when children are involved. Your digestive problems are chronic, but having a child put you over the edge. The mind is highly connected to the third chakra, and I'm sure that since becoming a father, your worrying has increased.

Combine that with your tendency to absorb, or digest, the pain of others, and that has caused your symptoms to worsen."

• • •

WHO'S AT RISK FOR AUTOIMMUNE DISEASES?

Reading energy is a big part of energy medicine. I find the third chakra to be one of the most expressive chakras in the body. What it represents is direct and incredibly useful when addressing most people's inability to love themselves.

In my experience, verbal, physical, and sexual abuse are the main reasons that people develop an autoimmune disease. A hole in the center of the chakra means that a person has been sexually abused; a dark ring around the chakra indicates verbal abuse; a jagged edge around the chakra signifies physical abuse; and sometimes a crater where the chakra is means self-abuse. Certainly, not everyone who has been verbally, physically, or sexually abused will develop an auto-immune disease, but these traumas could indicate a tendency toward immune weakness due to habitually weakened third-chakra energy. There have been times in my practice where a person has experienced significant trauma, but I don't see these symbolic metaphors. These people have done years of healing work on their past including therapy that literally cleans their energy of these traumas.

Having Problems with Your Digestion?

One way to support a healing digestive system is to avoid certain foods for a period of time. This will help heal inflammation in the intestines. Consider avoiding sugar, dairy, raw veggies and other uncooked foods for a while. These foods take more energy and extra enzymes to digest properly. Another popular food to avoid—to give your gut a rest— is wheat (or gluten). More and more people are developing gluten-sensitivity, but here in the United States the problem is greater. Gluten is added to so much food, including salad dressings, coating on potato chips, and peanut butter. Sensitivities to gluten can arise when you digest gluten (or others ingredients like dairy or sugar) numerous times a day. See if you can reduce your symptoms by avoiding wheat and gluten for one month. If your symptoms clear up, consider a wheat-free diet. Many people report that their autoimmune conditions recover remarkably when they stop eating wheat. Remember that there are many delicious grains free of wheat and gluten.

For more information about food sensitivities and dietary substitutions, visit wholelifenutrition.net.

Verbal abuse is common in our society, yet most people accept such abuse and refuse to recognize it as a problem. There are dozens of types of verbal abuse, from neglect—not answering or acknowledging another—to loud swearing or yelling at another person. Just turning on your TV and watching coaches "coach" athletes is a perfect way to witness verbal abuse—and mainstream society considers this behavior acceptable. I wonder if this is the case with Mark's digestive issues?

* * *

"Mark, do you think you're hard on yourself?"

"Yes."

Even though Mark's third chakra shows no signs of abuse, its craterlike appearance tells me that he mentally abuses himself. Mark's compassion and ability to feel others' emotions makes him feel responsible for the lives of other people, even strangers.

"Would you want your daughter to be hard on herself?"

"No, of course not."

"Perfect," I say, thrilled that he can easily understand what he wants for his daughter, even though he has yet to understand that he deserves the same peace.

"Mark, you are just as precious as your daughter. You are wonderful and perfect just as you are now. You deserve to feel those same feelings that you have for your child, but for yourself as well."

"Wow, I think it would be impossible to feel that way about myself. I adore my daughter."

"I understand. When she becomes an adult, would you want her to feel less adoration than what you and your wife feel for her now?"

"Certainly not!" Mark says.

"Even at this early stage of development, your daughter is modeling her energy after those with whom she spends the most time. Once she becomes a teenager, she will work just as hard to model her energy after her peers. The sooner you create genuine, loving feelings about yourself, she will naturally do the same for herself. Plus, she will continue to feel those feelings as an adult, even if you and Mary aren't near to remind her of how precious she is to you."

"So if I feel love toward myself as I do my daughter, she will pick up on that and think that's a normal way of thinking and feeling?"

"Exactly!"

"OK, I'm in, I will work on it."

"Great. I just want to point out that it wasn't until you understood that your daughter would benefit from your loving yourself that you got on board."

"I know, I thought about that. Old ways are hard to change."

• • •

Cultivating the Art of Self-Love

To attain real self-love, your experience must be authentic. Many times we may *think* we love ourselves, because every self-help book on the planet has told us so. For any idea or practice to have a lasting and genuine impact, our emotions must be connected to it.

The trick to feeling bona fide love for yourself is to think of something or someone whom you *love unconditionally*— perhaps a child, a beloved pet, or a magical part of the world. Unconditional love means that if your daughter keeps you up at night for months when she has colic as a baby, or wrecks your car when she's sixteen, you still love her to pieces and always will.

If it's a pet you're thinking of, you care deeply for it as you would your child. Even if this four-legged animal soiled the rug or bit your neighbor, you adore it and hope it has a long and happy life with you.

If it's a piece of land or body of water you're thinking of—a magical, faraway place, or a mountain you see every day from your car when crossing a bridge—you can be grateful for its existence and feel a warmth in your heart every time you visit it in person or in your mind.

Now feel how much you love this person, pet, or place, and let the feeling expand. Allow the emotion to grow, as if you were holding the object of your love. When you let yourself feel this unconditional love, you'll find that very little can hold you back from intense, profound emotions.

Now transfer these intense yet warm feelings into your body, but just for you. That's right, let the unconditional emotions of love you feel for someone or something else move into your body, and allow yourself to feel comfortable experiencing these feelings toward yourself. You are just as wonderful as the other people or places to which you direct your love. You, too, are a blessed and irreplaceable part of creation. You are amazing! Now let yourself feel that. Feel it every day just for a few moments. Feeling even a small amount of self-love every day can make huge changes in your life. Now you know how!

• • •

I recently met with Mark for a second session. I was a little worried that he might still be experiencing pain. I had talked with him on the phone four months after our first session, and he still had digestive pain and couldn't quite understand how to feel unconditional love toward himself. To my delight, at our second session he told me that his pain had decreased by 90 percent. He was still taking medication, but now it was working.

Mark told me that every day he had been practicing the art of unconditionally loving himself. As a result, he had started to pay attention to his inner dialogue and had begun replacing old negative tapes with more compassionate and appreciative language. He said he was feeling physically better and all areas of his life were improving. He was expanding his practice, and his wife, Mary, was now pregnant with their second child.

Mark had realized that agonizing over his patients or worrying too frequently about his daughter didn't serve the people he cared for—and the stress diminished his own well-being. In the future, he hopes self-loving thoughts and feelings will assist him in living free of antidepressants.

. . .

Exercises for the Third Chakra

The following exercises are for the third chakra and all the organs and systems it governs. They will help you to flow vital life-force energy into your body to support healthy mental thinking and feelings of self-love.

Self-Love To-Do List

1. **Indulge in positive self-care daily.** At least once a day, ask yourself: what is the most loving thing I can do for me right now? When you internalize this question, you might get an idea such as going for a walk, listening to your favorite music, or enjoying a nourishing treat.

2. **Appreciate your accomplishments daily.** When was the last time you appreciated yourself for filling up the gas tank, taking out the trash, or driving the kids to school? Living in a physical reality requires doing a lot of tasks that most of us take for granted

and rarely appreciate. Go ahead: smile at yourself and thank yourself for all that you do!

3. **Recite the self-love mantra daily.** As you fall asleep at night, repeat this kind message to yourself silently: *Every day and in every way, my self-love deepens. I'm a happy, healthy person, and I will always be successful.*

Here is a nightly prayer that you can say to your children as they are falling off to sleep. It will help them maintain or create a healthy immune system. I personally like to lie next to my kids in bed and rub their heads as I repeat positive affirmations to them, such as: *Every day and in every way your body works miraculously well, creating healthy cells, vitality and a wonderful life.*

Repeat this many times as your child falls asleep.

One-Minute Recharging

1. Stretch your arms straight out from your shoulders, as if you were a kid playing airplane.
2. Now rock your torso back and forth without moving your hips. This rocking motion moves your rib cage, which then rubs the third chakra, charging it with vital energy. It's as if you are washing the chakra.

The Mirror

1. Stand or sit in front of a mirror every day.
2. Make direct eye contact with yourself and say kind, loving words while maintaining eye contact for two to three minutes. Here are a few options of phrases you might say:
   - I'm learning to love this man (or woman) in the mirror.
   - I'm learning to be proud of the man (or woman) in the mirror.
   - I'm learning to believe that this man (or woman) in the mirror is amazing.
   - I love you and appreciate everything about you.
   - You are an incredible being, beyond my wildest dreams.

It's important that you actually feel what you're saying. If you have resistance toward liking yourself, then the exercise may create even more opposition. The first three phrases can be useful in getting comfortable with caring about yourself and reduce the tendency to avoid loving yourself.

●

This exercise is great for children too, because self-esteem is the foundation of a child's well-being and the key to success as an adult. When coaching your child to do this exercise, perhaps use words similar to: brilliant, beautiful, happy, talented, imaginative, and healthy. Have fun with your child. Try playing music or singing the words into the mirror. If you're a little uncomfortable doing the above exercise yourself, do it with your kids first and let them show you how.

5

Fourth Chakra

Giving and Receiving

MY NEW CLIENT ARRIVES LATE in the afternoon and is sitting in the living room on a puffy orange sofa—part of what is left of my furniture after I split up with my husband. I'm embarrassed about the mismatched furniture and empty space where the coffee table used to be. I'll fill it with new furniture soon, I promise myself. Everyone goes through this when they get divorced, right?

The client rises and briskly shakes my hand. "Elaine," is all she says. Apparently, she has no time to waste. She immediately begins explaining her reasons for coming. When she speaks about her double mastectomy, I see that she is the type of client who has an urgent need and doesn't have time for my scanning and questioning.

I take a deep breath and set aside memories of hospital scenes with breast cancer patients from my days as an oncology nurse. I ground myself further into the earth in order to become present with Elaine. A few moments later we both laugh about how lucky she is to never have to wear a bra again. She has no nipples, even after bilateral reconstruction surgery. Thankfully, she was diagnosed with stage I cancer, the least extensive kind, with no lymph node involvement.

But we quickly put our kidding aside. Elaine is in her forties with two young children, and she is terrified of having a recurrence of the cancer and not being around to watch them grow up. I wonder if her fear is an intuition or something else. Either way, I think to myself, Elaine knows and talks a lot about cancer. She's smart, but her knowledge seems like that of someone who has inundated herself with information and who frequently talks about it. Part of my work will be teaching her why she needs to stop obsessing about cancer.

"My friends have been telling me about you for a few years," says Elaine, "but . . . I had a bad experience with another energy worker who told me the cancer would return and that I'd die in four years. That was two years ago."

Ah . . . here is the "something else" about her cancer, I think to myself. No wonder she's obsessed with cancer; someone has told her she is going to die from the disease.

I, too, have told nearly a dozen people that I could see their life force leaving their body in a way that meant they would most likely pass away. I don't feel that way about Elaine.

"I'm sorry for everything you have gone through, and I thank you so much for trying energy medicine again and giving us an opportunity to work together. What are *your* thoughts about healing your body and staying well?"

Before Elaine answers, I sense desperation pouring into her aura and the entire living room.

"Marie, I can't die. I have to stay here for my kids," she says in a panicked tone, tears filling her eyes.

Elaine's hands are clenching in her lap. I reach out and gently squeeze them.

"I'm sure you are a hard worker and a determined person who takes charge when life gets difficult," I say. Elaine nods her head yes a few times. "What I'm about to say might seem difficult to understand, but it will be important for you to become neutral about many things in life, including whether you're going to live. When you desire something desperately, you create more desperation. In other words, you need to learn to let go and trust that all is well."

* * *

Fourth Chakra—Universal Love

The fourth chakra, or heart chakra, is located in the center of the upper chest and is about loving everything in the universe unconditionally. It is a deep emerald green, and it governs the heart, lungs, thymus gland, rib cage, breasts, circulation of blood and lymph fluid, hands, forearms, and upper back. Universal love means that everything in the universe is perfect exactly the way it is. Learning the heart chakra's wisdom of love rewards us with the ability to give and receive equally. When we are at peace with our needs, we can more easily perceive that each moment is a unique, powerful, and precise for our growth and evolution.

Becoming aware of universal love and integrating it into one's consciousness allows energy to move into the higher vibrational chakras. (The first three chakras are primal. They are about surviving in our three-dimensional world. As profound as those chakras are, they vibrate at a lower frequency than chakras five, six, and seven.) The heart chakra is the entrance to the higher-vibration chakras. The fifth chakra is about expressing truth, the sixth chakra is about becoming a multisensory being, and the seventh chakra is about connecting to spiritual awareness.

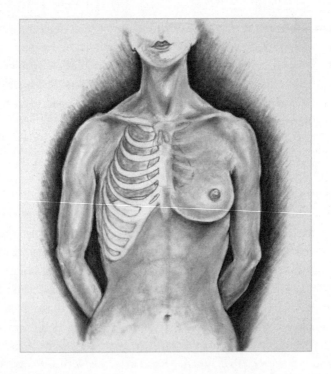

FIGURE 7. *The fourth chakra is the entryway to universal love. It is located in the upper chest, shown here in two views—one of the breast and one of the underlying anatomy.*

• • •

Elaine's case strikes me as a perfect example of fourth-chakra work. She briefly turns her head away from me, and her shoulder-length blond hair moves with her. I am intuiting thoughts through her aura that she is contemplating my words about her letting go of her fear of death. When she turns back and meets my gaze, her eyes are full of tears.

"I can't do that. I *have* to know I will be well so I can be there for my family." Several tears roll down her cheeks.

I hand her a tissue. "I know this will be the hardest thing I ask you to do, but I believe it's part of your personal work, one of the reasons you came to Earth this time. You're right that it won't be easy, but life lessons rarely are."

Elaine smiles and wipes away her tears. "The strange thing is I know you're right, Marie. I try too hard to make everything perfect. Deep inside, I know this exhausts me. Lately I have been wondering what perfection is and whether I'm qualified to determine that."

I stand and gesture for Elaine to move into my office. She enters the room ahead of me and quickly climbs on the tall massage table—again not wanting to waste any time. Despite our conversation, she looks comfortable and closes her eyes. I place one of my hands on her right shoulder and the other on her knee in order to ground her. Almost immediately, energy begins to smoothly run through Elaine's body from head to toe like a calm river flowing. Her energy system is available to me as if we are old friends. The movement is very positive—something I rarely experience the first time a client sees me. She lays her hands on mine, eyes still closed, and says, "I'm so happy to be here."

We talk about how being in flow is perfect, and how I believe that real perfection looks like an old-growth forest, with ferns growing on treetops in order to find light, and moss all over the ground, cushioning one's steps.

While scanning Elaine's energy, I notice energy leaking out of the back of her fourth chakra. This type of leak is common in those suffering from any disease located in the upper chest cavity. I ask Elaine questions in preparation for the homework I will assign her. The exercises will help her prevent energy from leaking after she leaves here. Elaine will need to learn how to maintain all of her energy, not just that of the heart chakra, to stay well.

"Elaine, you seem to know a lot about oncology treatments. Do you help others who are diagnosed with cancer?"

"Yes, I do. When I was diagnosed two years ago, I read everything I could on the subject. I want people who are newly diagnosed with cancer to have all the information possible to help them make the best choice."

"I appreciate that, Elaine. Thank you for helping so many people."

"Oh, it's my pleasure. Even people I don't know call me for help."

"Do you enjoy helping others?"

"Yes, very much."

"When you have finished talking to someone about cancer, or when you're helping another person in any way, do you feel invigorated?"

"I hadn't really thought about it that way. But now that you've asked, I would have to say no, I generally feel a little drained."

"Then I want you to stop. When we take right actions for ourselves, we are energetically fed by the activity. Whenever we feel drained, it's a sign that participating in those activities is not for our highest good."

"But I can't just stop helping others. I've done it my whole life."

"Elaine, you are leaking energy from the back of your fourth chakra. You don't have enough energy for yourself, let alone another."

• • •

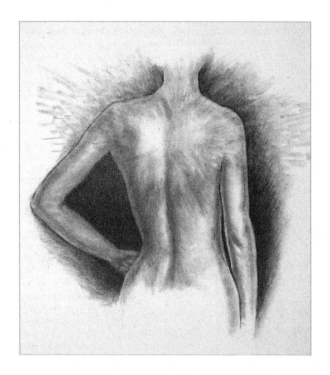

FIGURE 8. *The mate of the fourth chakra, located in the upper back, is the area of the body with the highest capacity to receive abundance.*

THE ART OF ALLOWING

The fourth chakra's mate receives the highest amount of energy in the human body. In its normal state, this chakra receives health, love, joy, and wealth. Many people refuse to receive, energetically blocking the back of their fourth chakra. I typically see large wooden or iron doors, like those from the Middle Ages, preventing the fourth chakra from receiving abundant energy. Other people, like Elaine, leak their vital life force from this chakra's mate. They leak in order to give to those people who they *feel* can't help themselves—giving their energy even to complete strangers.

The leaking, which is generally subconscious, devastates the anatomical structures in the chest: heart, lungs, breast tissue, thymus gland, lymph fluid, and blood vessels. It's very important for us all to realize that we're deserving of energy and an abundant life—even if others around us do not allow this for themselves. It takes energy to give, and it takes energy to refuse the kindness and giving nature of others. To truly receive is passive. When we let our beings and souls be fed by the world around us, then and only then can we give.

• • •

Elaine's energy moves in a familiar pattern of someone more concerned with others than herself.

"Elaine, your concern and care for others has gotten out of hand. You care so much that you unknowingly leak your vital life force from your body to give to others who you feel are less fortunate than you."

"OK, why is this bad?"

"It is just like the emergency instructions given on an airplane before takeoff—always put on your oxygen mask first before helping another, or you might pass out and be of no help to anyone. You need all of your energy. There is plenty of energy for everyone all the time. Most people don't take the energy given by others. Most of the energy you leak from your fourth chakra just hangs out in the ether, unused."

Elaine looks at me as if I have just spoken in a foreign language. "What do you mean, there is plenty of energy for everyone?"

"The universe is full of energy, and the supply is abundant and available to anyone who wishes to take it into their body at any time."

• • •

Everything Is Energy

The page you're reading right now is made up of trillions of subatomic particles. So is the ink. The subatomic particles, which are composed of electrons and protons, are continually in motion, forming images you can see and relate to with your human eyes. Everything in the universe is animated with energy. Quantum physics, the branch of science that studies subatomic particles, has helped us to understand why and how this is true.

The subatomic world of energy creates the home you live in, the car you drive, and the clothing you're wearing right now. Beneath the texture, design, and color of your clothing is another formation of subatomic particles—the human body. Your body pulsates with energy. With every breath, your body moves vast amounts of blood to your heart while cleansing carbon dioxide from your lungs. Your body is powered by millions of cellular energetic contacts.

Energy medicine is based on the laws of quantum physics—mass is energy. Even an object at rest has energy stored in its mass. These laws govern the human body and everything living within it: organs, tissues, bones, blood, cells, and DNA. If everything is made of energy, then diseases are too. Diseases occur in those areas of the body where energy is stagnant or barely moving. In contrast, healthy, vital areas of the body are full of motion of freely-circulating energy.

It's hard to imagine that everything in the universe is made of invisible tiny dots, which most people can see only with an electron microscope. If I didn't see that the world is composed of subatomic particles, I, too, would find it challenging to accept.

Thoughts and feelings are energy too. If our thoughts are consumed by worries and concerns, that's the type of energy that runs through our bodies. Stress is the leading cause of disease. Only by adopting a new philosophy that lets us see the beauty in each moment rather than the suffering will we be able to stop leaking our own precious energy and ultimately learn how to receive energy—the real job of the fourth chakra.

Most people learn through experiencing difficulties in their lives, because we generally choose to learn unconsciously: when we incarnate to Earth we forget our past lives and the lessons we want to learn while we journey here. Once we recognize the enormous free will we each possess, our past struggles become beautiful. As we learn to grow consciously, obstacles disappear and we are filled with gratitude.

Free Will

Free will is the greatest law that governs the universe. Even reincarnation takes an act of free will. Before reincarnating to Earth, we freely choose our gender and the parents we feel can offer us the greatest amount of learning. We also carefully choose the type of learning that will assist our soul's evolution and healing. In making these choices, we take our time and look at all the possible alternatives that allow this to happen, including choosing which century to incarnate in. The next time obstacles show up in your life and have you wondering, "Why is this happening to me?", remember divine will abounds and it's yours!

Realizing that each of us is responsible for our own life, we find out that there's another way to deepen our understanding of it that does not require suffering. Learning to do this takes time. Generally, people continue experiencing difficulty several times before their consciousness shifts to learning through positive actions and thoughts.

I'm not advocating that we ignore other people's pain; I'm suggesting that we can help them more if we can see possibilities instead of limitations. This will help others as well as ourselves. Instead of worrying about a situation, we need to shift our perception of it by asking our inner beings to show us the beauty in the obstacle. Wait, and then see what shows up for you.

• • •

In Elaine's case, I advise that she reserve the compassion she bestows upon other people with cancer for herself. She sheds a few tears. "It's so hard to watch others suffer that I don't think I can do what you're asking. I don't need that much care. I'm strong and have lived a comfortable life."

"That may be true, but you just survived cancer, a huge surgery, and toxic medication, and you now suffer from the fear that cancer will return."

I ask Elaine about her childhood, because feeling overly compassionate for others usually begins then. Elaine tells me that her father, a physician, worked many hours, and her mother, who stayed home with the children, was emotionally unstable. The four children had to care for themselves at times and constantly worried about their mother's welfare. Elaine says the situation was rarely discussed, even in adulthood. She believes her father felt guilty when she was young, but was never able to correct the situation.

"Elaine, I find it fascinating that you defended your father when telling me the story, but as a child you were a caretaker for your mother. I don't mean to criticize either one of your parents, but at some point you might need to admit that you were a child, and it was their responsibility, as adults, to care for you."

Elaine gently taps my hand, which is lying on top of her heart chakra, and says, "But I can feel his pain, and I don't want him to feel it."

"Have you ever told your father how you feel?"

"No, it would kill him."

I know Elaine's comment is an exaggeration, but I also know this is exactly how she tries to protect other people's feelings. "If he doesn't know how you feel, how will he learn? This is where you can benefit from feeling neutral about the situation. If you could stop feeling your father's feelings and instead be honest with him about your childhood, you both might grow from the experience."

I saw Elaine regularly over the next two years. During that time, she wasn't able to tell her father of her feelings about her childhood, nor was it easy for her to see the beauty in difficult situations. But she worked at it, asking me the same questions over and over, trying to gain a new perspective.

Then one day Elaine tells me that her disease has advanced from a stage I cancer that had been aggressively treated, to stage IV. Elaine now has a malignant tumor on a posterior rib, and because her cancer was estrogen positive, she has undergone a hysterectomy to slow its advance.

Elaine is clearly shaken and speaks about her oncologist, who she believes is as upset as she is. "My heart went out to him when he had to tell me the news. I know he thinks of me like a daughter, and the look on his face was devastating."

Knowing Elaine's oncologist, I'm sure her description of his feelings was accurate, but I want her to separate herself from him and connect to her own feelings. "What do *you* think about the new diagnosis?"

"Oh, it's disappointing. I thought I was in the clear. I did everything right, and now my cancer is at stage IV? But I know I will be all right. I just know it."

As Elaine speaks, I feel little emotion in her voice.

"Elaine, I want to point out that you're more connected to your oncologist's feelings than your own. I know you're an empathic person, but it's essential that you learn to feel neutral toward what others feel. Only then will your feelings take precedence over those of others. I believe that breast cancer is a disease of repressed grief. If you don't feel your grief, then you cannot release it. And unfortunately, if that happens, grief could continue to manifest as disease."

Elaine seems to be listening to me, but then goes on to talk about her mother's failing health and her worries about her aging parents, who still live in her childhood home. Her father refuses to move or find more help for her mother, yet he can't care for her on his own.

"I visit them often because I'm the only family member who lives nearby. I'm frustrated that my mom doesn't want to improve and that my father can't see that her health is growing worse."

"So, on top of your own health problems, you're caring for your mother?"

"When you put it like that, it sounds awful."

"Elaine, you need to set some boundaries. You're continuing to be the nurturer when now, more than ever, you need to be nurtured."

Elaine and I have talked many times about the grief buried in her body related to not being nurtured as a child, and how her empathy for others exacerbates it. I worry when a client's illness worsens, as Elaine's has. I know how hard it is to do inner work during the best of circumstances, and now that things are looking less than optimal for Elaine, it's even more difficult.

The rib cage is a great hiding place for unfelt emotions. Women generally store grief there, whereas men store repressed anger. After a while, if the anger or grief is not felt, the pent-up emotion will leak into the body and potentially cause disease to the surrounding areas of the heart chakra: the heart, lungs, breasts, and thymus gland.

Elaine sees the concern on my face and says, "What do you think? Are you worried about the new tumor?"

"I'm so sorry you have to go through all of this again—the surgery and all the treatments. You're a wonderful person and deserve to live your life free of health crises that interrupt it. But to really answer your question, I, too, know you will be well. Perhaps you will join the millions of Americans who are living with cancer."

"I think the very same thing, and I'm OK with that. Do you still see me dancing at one of my children's weddings?"

Elaine often asks me this question. The first day we met, a vision appeared to me just as I was internally questioning her future. I saw her wearing a light lavender dress and dancing at just such a wedding. I told her about my vision to calm her, because I could tell she worried that she would leave her body too soon.

"Yes, Elaine, I can still see the same vision. I do want to remind you that not all my visions come true. What's most important is that you become neutral about the outcome of your life," I said, explaining that truth to her again. "Anything can happen at any moment. I could be hit by a bus tomorrow and die many years before you. The length of one's life is less important than how one lives it."

• • •

Staying Neutral

Judging circumstances as good or bad means we want something specific to happen in order to be happy, blessed, lucky—or whatever it is that we seek as human beings. Even though we want something specific to happen, all situations are in fact the same. They just are. In each moment, there is more beauty than we can possibly stand. Letting go of our desires and judgments, and just allowing the beauty to be seen, is what "neutral" means. Being neutral is a high frequency that flows within the fourth chakra. It is from this unbiased place that we learn to forgive, to compromise instead of fight, and to love where originally we felt there was nothing to love. This place, deep within the fourth chakra, is where real peace lives. Gaining access to this type of love allows human beings to grow consciously.

● ● ●

Elaine has difficulty grasping this. "Logically I know what you're saying, Marie, but emotionally I can't seem to get out of my fear of dying," she tells me.

"Elaine, we are all dying—emotionally, spiritually, and physically—all the time. This is how we evolve. If we worry about the tiny deaths that happen each day, or the final one we most fear, how can we truly live? It's important to live in the moment—this moment, not some future unknown moment dredged up out of fear. You are a mom, wife, daughter, friend, and human being *right now*. This is your moment. This is all there is."

Are You an Empath?

Human beings have been collectively evolving the idea of self-love (third chakra). What does self-love look like and how can I know that I've attained it? If you have worked on loving yourself, you might think it's a daunting task, one that you'll labor at for years. But here's some good news! The human race has reached the tipping point about becoming emotionally aware of self-love, which means that as a group we will be spending more time in the fourth chakra. This means that more and more people will open their hearts and care for others. The fourth chakra will literally expand in size and many people will become empathetic. To be empathic means to feel the feelings of others, even those of complete strangers.

Empathy is a gift that will lead us to feed, clothe, and support our world in ways we have yet to imagine. The challenge of being empathic is to become comfortable with the feelings of others—even when others are sad, lonely, or distressed—and remain dedicated to their emotions and life.

Elaine left my office that day more determined to stay present and happy with what is. She read and listened to positive messages and practiced affirmations daily to stay away from fear. Her conventional treatments went very well, and within a year her cancer was in remission again. Elaine experienced few side effects from her treatments and was able to successfully use a new drug that strengthens bones, rather than drugs that repress the immune system, to stop the progression of tumors. I told her this was a good sign, and that she was learning to live with less fear.

"Our outer world is a reflection of our inner world," I say. "You must be nurturing yourself more these days, because your treatments are less harsh on your body than your previous treatment. How have you been able to nurture yourself?"

"Well, it's been challenging, but I convinced my father to hire in-home health care workers for Mom. But I ended up coordinating their schedules because my mother kept firing them."

I try not to chuckle as Elaine talks about her mother, who is growing weaker while still wielding power over others. I had never met her parents, but have had many visions of them, their home, and her mother's manipulative behavior pattern.

"So let me get this straight. Your dad lets your mom make decisions about her health care, but he won't coordinate them? Have you thought about setting a boundary with your dad, because I'm seeing several caregivers whose firing wasn't necessary."

"I knew you were going to say that; but all of this is so hard on my father, and he finally agreed to in-home care, and I want to make sure that my suggestion works for all of us."

"The real challenge is for you to learn how to feel your feelings and be neutral about others," I remind her.

Elaine still has difficulty feeling her own feelings more than the feelings of others. She remains unable to talk with her father about her childhood, and she continues to worry about his happiness. Shortly after she successfully organized her mother's move into an extended-care facility, her mother passed away. Elaine has been a client for ten years now, and is successfully living with cancer. She continues to learn more about herself and knows that none of us can control our lives and still grow. She focuses on having fun dancing wherever she is.

• • •

Healing Exercises for the Fourth Chakra

The following exercises are for the fourth chakra and all the organs and systems it governs. They will help you learn how to receive, become neutral, and expand to higher vibrational chakras to speak your truth, become a multisensory being, and connect to source energy.

One-Minute Balance

This simple exercise helps reduce anxiety and quickly balances the fourth chakra by aligning it with universal love. Use several fingers to gently tap your mid-sternum for one minute. This exercise activates the thymus gland, which plays an important role in balancing our immune system, increasing energy levels, and improving blood circulation. (If your stress is highly elevated, tap for several minutes.)

Receiving Energy

The back of the fourth chakra is between the shoulder blades. This area of the body has the highest receptivity to energy. To balance the heart chakra, you can visualize or feel energy moving into your back at least five times a day. For example, you could visualize a large flock of birds flying into your back, hear or feel warm rain moving into your back, or hear a wonderful melody vibrating and filling up the heart chakra.

A great way to practice receiving love is to stand in the shower with your back facing the spray of water.

People who can most benefit from this exercise often tend to forget to do it. A great way to remember is to pay attention when others acknowledge you in a positive way—perhaps when someone says, "Thank you!" or "Cute shirt!" or "Have a great day!" Let these moments of kindness remind you to receive through the heart chakra.

Once you get the hang of this exercise, it's important to feel the act of receiving, which can often be an enormously moving experience.

•

Children have great imaginations and can easily learn how to receive energy into their backs. When your children are dreaming of wonderful possibilities about what they will do when they grow up, encourage them to imagine their future careers moving into their backs. This practice will attract the necessary energy to make their dreams a reality.

Experiencing Beauty in All Things

It takes an open mind and heart to see beauty in all things. Practicing such openness lets us hold universal love in our hearts and minds. Following are two meditations that erase fearful thoughts and negative judgments, helping you feel a more expansive love. If you're not sure whether you tend to judge or just think negative thoughts, pay attention to your thoughts for a couple of days. You might be surprised with what you discover.

Breathing Meditation

The next time you hear of a horrifying event about which you think nothing positive can be said, try this exercise to quiet your worry and fear. Find a quiet place to sit alone and breathe deeply for five minutes. Then follow this simple Zen breathing meditation for five minutes:

1. Sit in a comfortable position and gently close your eyes.
2. Take a few deep breaths, and then breathe naturally without consciously trying to control it.
3. Count "one" as you exhale.
4. Inhale, and then count "two" when you next exhale, and so on to "five."
5. Then begin a new cycle of counting your breaths from one to five.

Walking Meditation

If sitting isn't relaxing for you, try going on a walking meditation. Choose a nearby park or beach and walk for thirty minutes, inhaling and exhaling in time with your walking.

After the exercises have calmed you, revisit the disturbing images and information in your mind, and ask yourself whether there is any meaning or beauty in the situation. I recently did this exercise following Japan's tsunami and nuclear disaster. I was reminded of how I was filled with hope when I read about the compassion the Japanese people showed one another: people living in other provinces conserved energy to provide more resources to the devastated area, sometimes using candles instead of electricity. The city government of Tokyo changed their work hours to earlier in the day to avoid using electricity when it became dark. There was no looting in the streets or riots. I truly felt the Japanese people, in their tragedy, offered teachings for all of us to follow. And I was truly grateful.

You might initially discover a new way of looking at the situation, or you might need to meditate again to feel less distressed. Rest assured, there is always beauty in everything.

Learning Not to Judge Others

Many of us judge others because of their gender, race, economic state, or clothing choices. This exercise teaches you how to love instead of judge.

When you find yourself in a public place with many people, find something to appreciate about some of them. Maybe you can appreciate a hairstyle, a coat, or the way a person holds a child's hand. Genuinely feeling your appreciation of these simple things can reduce your negative thinking.

When we see beauty in anything, it makes it easier to see the beauty within ourselves.

6

Fifth Chakra

Speaking Your Truth

MY CLIENT JULIE HAD SEEN me for a few years for help with minor health concerns related to a stressful marriage to an alcoholic. A forty-something mother of four, she is trying her best to maintain a relationship with her ex-husband because of their children.

Sitting in a chair in my office, Julie is the epitome of health. She's in great physical shape from exercising regularly and taking care of her appearance. Her long, blond hair shines in the sunlight coming through the window. Her youngest child, Sarah, is lying on the massage table. Though only eight years old, Sarah is an amazing athlete like her three older brothers. She competes at the state level in gymnastics and was training for a big championship when she developed pain in her right elbow about a month ago which prevented her from continuing.

Her pediatrician hadn't found any fractures or other structural problems on her X-rays. A Doppler ultrasound, which measures blood as it flows through vessels, did show decreased blood flow in her elbow but the specialist at a children's hospital had no idea what caused it. He recommended that Sarah not use her arm for four weeks, after which he would recheck the blood flow. Sarah's appointment was coming up in ten days, and she was still experiencing pain. Julie thought I might be able to help.

Sarah is adorable. I can tell she is a good person, and her mother looks so proud of her. I feel overwhelming compassion for their family because they've been through such a difficult time. I know that participating in athletics is the best way they've found to cope with the stress; Sarah's older brothers are all competitive divers. A vision comes to my mind of Julie and her children attending sporting events and supporting one another. It's their way of bonding. I also see a vision of little Sarah surrounded by her big brothers, who definitely love her but also treat her like one of the boys, making her compete a little at home too.

I explain the chakra system to Sarah as I do to all children, focusing on the chakras' colors and how they rotate. I ask if I can lay my hands on her. She says yes. She looks excited, as if she thinks what I do is a mystery, but one that she looks forward to experiencing.

I'm immediately drawn to Sarah's right elbow, even though Julie has not told me which one hurts. I'm also drawn to the right side of her neck. Whether the two are connected I don't yet know, but I'm certain the fifth chakra is involved. As I touch Sarah's elbow, a blue line that runs from her elbow to her throat appears in my mind.

"Does this hurt, Sarah?"

"A little."

"I'm sorry. I will do my best not to cause you any pain that hurts more than this. Just tell me to stop whenever you want me to . . . OK?"

"She's tough and can handle it," Julie says. "Right, honey?"

"Yes, it's not bad. I'm fine."

"OK then, I'm going to push in this area for a little bit longer, but without any more pressure than this. Is that OK?" Sarah smiles at me and says yes.

As I apply pressure, I see Sarah's gymnastics coach in my mind. I see a man about forty years old, wearing navy sweatpants, a white T-shirt, and a red zip-up jacket. He's almost six feet tall and is standing next to a balance beam in a very large gym. A young girl is walking, or more like dancing, on the beam. The coach is yelling at her. The young girl is Sarah.

"Do you like gymnastics, Sarah?"

"Yes, very much!"

"Do you like your coach?"

"Yes."

Before I explain my vision, as I do in every session, I look at Julie to see if she has reacted to my question. Her face hasn't changed.

"Well, I see your coach yelling at you. Is that true?"

Julie squirms a little in her chair and says, "He's very talented, and Sarah is lucky to have him as a coach. But yes, he can be difficult."

"Oh. Is that OK with you, Sarah?"

"Yes."

"Well, here is what I think. The lack of blood flow to Sarah's elbow is directly linked to her coach's behavior. Yelling doesn't help anyone perform well. Besides, Sarah is a good kid. She follows direction well and truly wants to please others."

Julie says, "We know he can be challenging, but he's one of the best coaches in the area, and Sarah loves competing. It's unusual for someone as young as Sarah to compete at the state level and win."

I look down at Sarah's face and smile. I see her on the uneven bars. She's flying through the air after letting go of the high bar. I'm sure only seconds pass before she grabs the low bar, but in my vision, she's soaring in slow motion. I can see her strong and well-developed muscles as she extends her legs behind her and reaches out in front with both hands, preparing for contact with the low bar. I feel her adrenaline as her muscles tighten and her hands slap and grab the low bar. Chalk sprays in the air and off she goes again.

Sarah's athletic abilities inspire me. I can also admire Julie for keeping her kids in sports, given all the time constraints, costs, and difficult personalities of some coaches. My ex-husband coached all three of our daughters' soccer teams. He yelled. I hated it. After a while, he realized that to keep me from giving him *the look* every five minutes, he needed to end each sentence to the girls with "honey."

I realize that Julie might not be sensitive to Sarah's feelings. And Sarah has learned to keep her feelings under wraps. With three older brothers, her coach, and an alcoholic father, this little girl is showing signs that it's difficult for her to speak her truth.

• • •

Fifth Chakra — Personal Power

The fifth chakra is located in the center of your throat and is light blue. This chakra governs the throat, mouth, teeth, gums, tongue, tonsils, thyroid gland, cervical vertebra, voice box, esophagus, elbows, forearms, and shoulders. On an emotional level, this chakra is about speaking your truth. When we speak our truth, we empower ourselves. Power isn't about feeling better than another or taking advantage

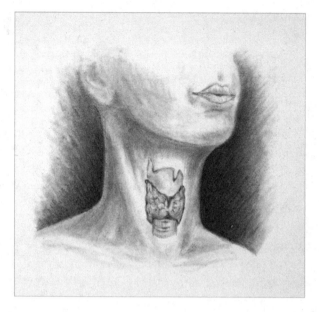

FIGURE 9. *The fifth chakra helps you express your truth and is located near the thyroid gland and trachea.*

of another, which is how our culture defines it. True power is about feeling safe enough to be vulnerable.

Feeling the Essence of Your Personal Power

Sometimes it's difficult to understand how powerful we really are. Here is a meditative exercise to help you feel your inner power.

Close your eyes and take several deep breaths to relax your body. Imagine that beautiful roots or vines are growing out of your feet and into the floor, grounding you to the earth. As you inhale, breathe in tranquil energy. As you exhale, release any stress that you have experienced during the day, week, or month. After a few minutes of calmly breathing, bring your awareness to a tiny spot of light deep in your body. Let your being become very small, as small as the tiny spot of light. How does it feel to be this small? How does it feel to contract your existence into the minute brightness? Gently allow your daily activities to disappear. Only allow those thoughts in that can fit into the clear light. Feel the ease of being so small and let all other things flow away from your attention. Stay in this place for several minutes, getting to know your personal power to contract your energy.

Now allow the light to expand. Let your being get bigger and bigger and bigger. The light surrounds your entire being stretching out past the walls of the room you're sitting in. Within the enlarged light, feel your being soar beyond any boundaries as you become acquainted with the limitless being you truly are. How does it feel to be so big? So far away? Nothing is holding you back as you magically grow. Feel the sensation of being large for several minutes, and then when you're ready, return to the room within the natural boundary of your human world and feel how grounded your feet are to the earth.

* * *

I decide to follow my intuition about Sarah's fifth chakra.

"Sarah, what's it like to be the youngest in your family?"

"I like it."

"Do you and your brothers roughhouse?"

Sarah and her mother chuckle, then her mother says, "Yes."

"I bet."

I see all three boys in my head: strong, funny, and definitely independently minded. I hear words accompanying the vision: "Everyone in this family needs to be strong. There's no room for displays of weakness."

"Do you tell your brothers how you feel?"

"Not really. I try, but if I cry, they call me a baby." I keep steady pressure with my finger on a spot at the inside of her elbow that is highlighted in my mind. The pressure eventually releases large amounts of stagnant energy that pours out of her elbow and into the room.

Sarah's mother says, "Sometimes they can be mean." She makes a sad face to show Sarah her sympathy.

"And I guess talking with your coach about how his yelling is affecting you is out of the question?"

"My mom talked with him a couple times, but he doesn't understand that he's yelling."

"That can definitely be a challenge." I remember all too well my ex-husband's sideline roar.

"Well, Sarah, it looks like saying how you feel is an issue in a few areas of your life. Let's first get the blood flowing in your elbow so you can compete soon, while you learn to feel comfortable saying how you feel." I pause for a moment. "Instead of telling others how you feel, do you think you could write down your feelings in a notebook?"

Sarah lifts her head off the table and looks at her mother, who smiles and nods yes.

"OK," Sarah says.

"Great, I'm glad we have a plan. Making sounds with your voice is the best way to release stagnant energy from the fifth chakra, but any way you can express real emotion will help the fifth chakra and ultimately your elbow."

They both look happy. Even the room feels warm with their new plan. Over the years I have noticed that expressing words can change an entire situation, including the energy in a room. I feel confident that Sarah will be able to compete.

• • •

TRUE POWER OPENS YOUR SOUL

When people speak their true emotions, I see an energy heat wave caused by thousands of subatomic particles moving into the front of their fifth chakra. This energy comes from the soul. Your soul knows all things and resonates only with truth. When we avoid our truth or lie, we leak vital life-force energy from the fifth chakra, potentially causing illness in the structures the chakra supports.

Most people avoid their truth—smiling when they're not happy, telling others they're fine when they're actually heart-broken, broke, mad, or sick. Stranger still, many people hide feelings of happiness so as not to make others uncomfortable. In fact, most people repress their emotions so strongly that they push them deep within their body, creating stagnant energy and weakening their energy system.

It's empowering to tell another (or even yourself) what you really feel. When others know what you're actually feeling, they have an opportunity to know the real you and can

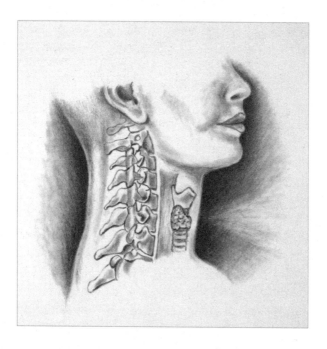

FIGURE 10. *Empowering energy moves into the area where the fifth chakra is located: the cervical vertebrae, thyroid gland, and esophagus.*

better nurture you in a way that supports your individuality. If someone doesn't understand you or can't foster support, that's information that could help you make healthy choices about whom you want to have in your life. When you learn to speak your truth, you access and strengthen its power to set you free.

Those who embody personal power are unconcerned with what others think of them. This is one of the greatest gifts you can give yourself. True power is kind. It doesn't judge others, yet it understands that to harness authentic power, you must embrace and express your true self.

• • •

Because they carry less emotional baggage than adults, most children heal quickly. They easily grasp teachings, such as the theory of personal power. When parents reinforce these new ideas, the integration can last a lifetime. However, when parents are learning the same concept as their child, their reinforcement is weak and the concept may dissipate.

After two sessions, Sarah's blood flow to her elbow returned to normal, and all of her pain disappeared, and she returned to competitive gymnastics. She expressed that my insights about her coach were valid. The journaling was helpful and she felt more relaxed at home and in the gym.

Two years later, Sarah came to see me again, complaining of the same symptoms. During the session, we returned to the conversation about her coach's style and how emotionally hard it is for Sarah to cope with. I told her that her feelings were getting trapped in her body, causing pain and other physical symptoms.

When I looked at Sarah and her mother during that session, I knew that they had been talking about Sarah making some changes about her sport. A few days after Sarah left the office, she decided to switch sports. She joined her brothers in their passion—competitive diving. She told me later that her new diving coach was nice and hardly yelled. I was thrilled.

I didn't see Sarah again for six years. She's now sixteen years old and quite attractive. She returned because of a benign growth on her thyroid.

By now quite comfortable in my office, Sarah plops on the table.

"So, my dear, your thyroid is telling you what your elbow has been saying for years," I say.

"I know. The doctors want me to have surgery, but I absolutely don't want a scar. Mom and I thought you could do your magic."

I smile at both of them. They are both so cute . . . literally. I'm also thinking, "Ladies, how about *doing inner work?*"

Instead, I say, "Let me take a look at your thyroid gland and see what comes up for me."

I place my right hand above Sarah's throat and my left on her right shoulder to ground her to the earth. My right hand is about three inches above the gland. The energy that comes off her thyroid is intense. It feels as it does when I have held my cell phone on my ear far too long . . . almost painful. At the same time that I'm feeling this intensity, I also see problems with the biopsy. I have a vision of a doctor in scrubs with a mask, just finishing a needle biopsy of Sarah's thyroid. He hands the syringe to a nurse standing near him. On top of his head appears a question mark about three feet tall. My mind zeroes in on the question mark.

"Sarah, you said the growth is benign, but did the biopsy raise questions for the doctors?" Sarah looks up at her mother, who raises an eyebrow.

"Yes, they're not 100 percent sure the growth is benign. They weren't able to get enough cells and don't want to do another biopsy in case it's cancer. If it is, they don't want to disturb the area."

I spend more time in the area using every trick in my toolbox to get the energy to change. I use Reiki symbols, and other modalities I commonly practice. I set a positive attention of health in the area. I ask for divine light to emerge into her thyroid gland and invite her body to absorb the perfect energy it needs to facilitate a shift in her thyroid. Despite this, there is no recognizable change. I know what I have to tell Sarah and her mother, but I continue doing energy work on the area before I explain my findings.

After a few minutes, I say, "Well, I think the growth is most likely benign, but I do think the cells are changing. They are beginning to resemble pre-cancer cells. Luckily, if there's cancer in the thyroid, it rarely spreads to other parts of the body. But I feel you need to have the surgery. If you don't wait too long, I'm hoping the surgeon can save some of your thyroid. Then you might be able to avoid taking prescription drugs to regulate your hormones."

Both Julie and Sarah look surprised. They didn't expect this recommendation from me.

"You don't think that the growth can go away on its own?"

"I do think the growth can go away or stop growing if Sarah works on understanding why it's hard for her to express her feelings. But this type of self-reflection takes time. The tumor feels aggressive to me. I'm looking at what is the healthiest course of action based on her history at this time."

I can feel Sarah's anxiety about the surgery and her mother's desire to avoid any potential pain or side effect from an invasive procedure. Julie and Sarah glance at one another many times, letting me know the high level of anxiety that our conversation is causing.

I know Sarah has had a few health issues connected to her throat chakra, indicating that she has yet to identify her authenticity.

"Getting to know your truth, Sarah, is a personal experience. Your reality is based on your individual feelings, because each of us reacts to life differently. Many times we repress our truth because we unconsciously fear that others won't love us if we express ourselves genuinely. Getting past the fear is what will empower you. Your truth is a gift to humanity. If you reveal yourself, others will learn from your unique interpretation of life, and you will free yourself in the process."

"How can we help her to express herself?" Julie asked.

"First, it's important to realize that Sarah has a big heart and wants to please everyone. She feels the feelings of others very deeply, so she holds back her words so as not to hurt anyone. Sarah, you will need to put aside your sympathetic feelings and express yourself despite what you pick up about what others are feeling."

"Wow, I think that's right, Marie. Sarah comes and sits with me when I'm sad although I've said nothing about my feelings to her."

Sarah sits up on the table. She sheds a few tears. Her mom gets up and wipes them away and kisses her forehead.

"I'm not sure I can do what you're asking."

"I know." I smile and gently rub Sarah's left knee. "Give it a try, and if it takes longer than you expected, then you still have surgery as an option." I smile again and wink, this time to tease her, even though they both know I'm serious about the surgery. "There are many creams on the market that prevent scarring after surgery, Sarah," I say.

* * *

Strength through Vulnerability

When you're truly open, you're vulnerable, just like when you get a scrape on the knee. You may want to cover it up with a big bandage, but without fresh air the scrape will only get gooier. It can take a lot of courage to say what you really think and feel. And doing that doesn't mean the person to whom you're speaking will agree or understand you. Getting someone to agree with you is not the purpose of speaking honestly.

Instead, it lets others see who you are, what you want, and when you're willing to compromise. They get to know the real you—that's vulnerability. Real friends, partners, and family members are those who see one another for who they are and love who they see. They value your truth.

● ● ●

A year after my consultation, Sarah had surgery to remove the growth on her thyroid. The surgeon was able to save part of the gland, and she currently takes medications to supplement its natural function. She is hoping that her thyroid will adjust so she won't need the medications in the future. Sarah is now a more outspoken person: she will even yell at her siblings on occasion, when that seems necessary to be heard, and she takes pride in asking her coaches to respect her by using kind language. She is a sophomore and diver at a Texas university.

Julie describes her daughter today as a generous truth speaker. Sarah's honesty and kindness have helped her whole family grow and respond to one another more positively. Julie was surprised when I asked if I could use Sarah's story for the book, given that Sarah ended up needing surgery and medication to heal. I told Julie that the way we find healing doesn't matter—only that we heal.

What I was telling Sarah had resonance for me personally. After ending a marriage that had very little truth in it, I made a family rule for myself and my children: no matter what you're feeling, please share *your* truth. Learning to express your deepest fears and greatest joys builds confidence until you feel safe enough to be vulnerable. In our family, we've come to really know one another, both in our roles as family members and, more importantly, as friends. My daughters are now grown, and we all love to spend time together because we can each be ourselves with one another. As a parent I've received an extra bonus from letting my children speak honestly: I've learned from their clear insight. I believe that children are our best teachers.

• • •

The Power of Honesty

If you want to have honest relationships so you and others get to know the real you, here are some helpful guidelines. I've added a few stories to help you better understand.

1. Truth can be painful. Ultimately, pain will be replaced by spectacular feelings of freedom, because the pain of grief is a gateway to a new way of being.

   Before my marriage ended, my ex-husband and I were doing our best to move through the muddy waters of changing a relationship. To our utter shock, I was learning to speak my truth, and it wasn't going over very well. He wanted to know where the old me had gone, and I was surprised every day by what was coming out of my mouth. With each conversation, it became increasingly obvious that we were no longer in agreement about most things. This awareness deeply disturbed me, but I wasn't willing to return to my old behaviors and stifle my feelings to keep the peace. To ease my anxiety, I began to meditate and discovered a much-needed connection with myself, which continues to give me peace even today.

2. As you honestly express yourself, the real you will magically appear.

Before ever teaching a class, I organized a group with friends to better learn the art of manifesting and to practice my teaching skills. We would also regularly meditate. During one of our meditations, I saw myself standing on a stage speaking to several hundred people. I felt so happy during this visualization but also confused. Talking in front of just a few people was challenging for me. I would turn red and get really hot and perspire—not a pretty picture for a speaker. Yet I could not shake the thought of how much fun I was having in my vision. So I let myself enjoy the vision regularly. Inside, I felt that the universe was helping me grasp something about myself. Of course, today I speak to thousands of people via classes, radio programs, and this, my first book.

3. Get ready for a change, because your life will change.

At one point in my nursing career, I began to notice that stepping out of the hospital at the end of my shift and into the light of day brought me joy and a feeling of relaxation. I took this as a sign that working as a nurse had become stressful. I was overcome with grief because I loved nursing.

I also worried about my future. I had worked hard to create my nursing career and worried about how I would make a living in the future if I left. However, in being honest with myself and expressing my feelings, I realized how much I wanted to work from home. I had not allowed myself to imagine this desire. The realization led me to learn about one of my greatest passions—energy work. I eventually created an energy medicine practice in which I could work at home, as I still do today.

EXERCISES FOR THE FIFTH CHAKRA

The following exercises are for the fifth chakra and all the organs and systems it governs. They will help you learn how to authentically express yourself and to become a powerful being. Take the speaking your truth quiz first, to evaluate how you speak your truth.

Quiz: Are You Speaking Your Truth?

There are four statements on page 104 that will help you gauge how well you speak your truth. Give yourself one to four points (as indicated in the scale below) based on how strongly the statements describe you.

1	This isn't true of me.
2	This may be true of me.
3	I want this to be true of me, and I'm working on it.
4	This is totally true of me, and I love how it feels!

I have a unique outlook on life _____
I share my unique outlook openly with others _____
I'm at peace if others don't understand my
   outlook _____
I realize that my unique outlook on life is valuable
   and helps others to grow and launch their own
   unique outlook _____

Now add up your points and read the corresponding paragraph for information about how well you express yourself now, and for a little hint on what to do next.

Points	Are You Speaking Your Truth?
4–6	You may understand the importance of speaking from your heart, but you have yet to do so. Practice speaking to objects that don't talk back: cats, rocks, walls. These things can become your new best friend when it comes to learning the art of powerful expression. After a while, you will notice a change in your energy that will give you the confidence to keep progressively sharing the real you with those in your life.
7–9	You're starting to share your genuineness. It may feel odd to do so, and your friends may think you've changed, but eventually the odd feeling will be replaced by an "aha" feeling. This lets you know that full expression is important, and striving to be fully expressive is your desired goal. Try to find one confidant—maybe someone you're not that close to—and practice a greater level of truth sharing with them. The experience will give you such a high energetically that soon words of truth will flow from you.

Points	Are You Speaking Your Truth?
10–13	You're sailing through life, authentically expressing yourself! Some friends may seem to have forgotten your address, but you're OK with it. You have met a few folks who share your worldview, and you know that new true friends are around the corner. You're grateful for your courage, and you feel free to be you! Pay close attention to the wisdom you're sharing; take notes, because your truth is meant to assist your evolution too.
14–16	You're an old hand at expressing your truth. Others flock to you for advice, and you can feel the power of your words reflecting out into the world. You have patience with those learning, or refusing to learn, this empowering privilege. You know that divine power is in each of us. You may consider teaching, counseling, or writing to further express yourself and your unique worldview.

One-Minute Balancing

To open your throat chakra and receive empowering energy, begin speaking out loud in a made-up language using guttural sounds. Do this exercise for one minute every day. When speaking in harsh tones, you will release pent-up energy from when you held back words that you thought might hurt another. Don't be surprised if your neck pain goes away or your thyroid functions better; this exercise is effective for both.

Over the years, I have discovered that people who shy away from this exercise really need to do it. If you felt uncomfortable reading about the quiz above, then close your book right now, find a quiet room, and yell in a made-up language. It will forever change your life.

This is a great exercise for parents with bickering offspring. My mother routinely suggested this exercise when any of her five children were shouting at the other. Every time we did the exercise, we burst out laughing instead of yelling at one another.

Toning for the Fifth Chakra

Several years ago, I began toning, creating a sound vibration, during sessions to increase the frequency of the energy work. I was a little embarrassed at first to make odd sounds come out of my mouth, especially since I'm tone deaf. But I know that sound carries exceptional vibration, and vibration can change any given situation. Toning affects our mood just the way music does, and that in turn transforms our energy. Follow these simple instructions to generate healthy energy in your fifth chakra:

1. Take a deep breath and slightly open your mouth.
2. Place the tip of your tongue on the roof of your mouth, anywhere that feels comfortable. Resting the tip of your tongue on the roof of your mouth stimulates Kundalini energy that then runs up and down your spine, increasing your overall energy. (See page 35 for more information about Kundalini energy.)
3. Make noise through your mouth; it may feel as if you are humming.
4. When you run out of breath, take another deep breath and repeat the sound with your tongue on the roof of your mouth.
5. Tone for a few minutes at a time; be sure to breathe.

When you feel genuinely empowered by using your voice, your being can soar! You will be better equipped to trust your intuition and create a healthy relationship with your sixth chakra, which is discussed in the following chapter.

— 7 —

Sixth Chakra

Becoming a Multisensory Being

Looking around my new office, I see that my mother's portable massage table fits perfectly, and the natural light that fills the room is warm and inviting. Just a month ago I was beside myself. As my divorce proceeding progressed, the court ordered me to return to the hospital and work full-time as a nurse. While married, I had been blessed to be able to work part-time, which allowed me to spend more time caring for our three daughters. Before the divorce, I had reduced my hours at the hospital, working as an on-call nurse and seeing clients out of my home. Everything was moving along perfectly, but I wasn't making enough money to support the girls—the reason behind the judge's order.

Just a few weeks ago, I explained my dilemma to one of my clients, an osteopath, and she immediately offered me a space to work at her clinic near my home. I graciously accepted. Before I knew it, her patients were banging on my door to schedule sessions. I managed to be at home one day a week so I could be available to my girls. Within two weeks of being offered the space, I requested a leave of absence from the hospital. I was already working full-time in my practice and earning more money than I had as a nurse, so I had satisfied the court's request.

Today, I am seeing one of the osteopath's patients—a twenty-two-year-old woman who dropped out of medical school because of debilitating seizures or "spells," as she calls them. They were not the grand mal seizures most people imagine, but more like brain activity overloads that left her mentally and physically exhausted. So far no treatment had worked to stop the seizures, and on some days she experienced multiple episodes.

As I sit in my office with the door ajar, a woman pokes her head in. She has a bright, shining face with big brown eyes. "Are you Marie?"

"Yes," I answer affectionately, thinking of all the welcoming faces over these last two weeks.

"Hi, I'm Bridget," she says, stepping cautiously into my office. "Thank you for seeing me. I know I'm a bit of a mess right now, but neither I nor the doctors know what to do. I had two seizures this morning. They're so unpredictable. So far I've been really lucky and haven't had any accidents or injuries when one occurs."

I can't stop looking at Bridget's dark hair and thick natural curls. I've always wanted hair like that. I sense that she doesn't feel the same way about her hair. In fact, as I listen to her, I have a strong feeling that she's having a hard time knowing who she is and that she's trying to be someone she's not.

"My first seizure happened two years ago just before I entered med school. While vacationing in Europe my 'spells' increased in intensity over the next month or so until I had a grand mal seizure. It happened in the middle of the night. I woke up on the floor tangled up in my sheets. I had bitten my tongue really hard. A French doctor told me I had dysentery and recommended homeopathic drops.

"I came back to Seattle immediately and went to a neurologist at the University of Washington who recommended EEG readings, which measure brain wave activity. Both the EEG and a CT scan showed that my brain was functioning normally. So the doctors couldn't treat me with conventional anti-seizure drugs. I had some chiropractic work done, rested, and the spells subsided for a while. I thought I was in the clear. Then three weeks into my first quarter in med school—wham—they came back with a vengeance. I'm glad I never had another grand mal seizure, but I had a lot of spells, and a rough scholastic ride. I dropped out after my first quarter."

"It must be very frustrating to have worked so hard for something only to walk away because of health problems," I say.

"Yes, I did my undergraduate degree at Stanford and then was accepted into medical school. I had thought about medicine as a career path, and when my father was diagnosed with cancer, the idea became even more attractive. He has now passed away, which was very difficult for me."

I release a quiet breath, feeling Bridget's family's shock and grief about her dad's passing. I instantly know that he was the rock of the family, a very smart and ambitious man. The entire family had a hard time coming to terms with his death, but his illness isn't a good reason for her to become a doctor. "I'm sorry to hear that your father is gone, Bridget. When your seizures go away, are you planning to return to medical school?"

Bridget looks intently into my eyes, seeming surprised by my question, and then says, "Absolutely."

That's it. When Bridget says, "Absolutely," the room instantly feels heavy, as if high-pressure clouds are accumulating into my small office, threatening rain. I realize it will be difficult for Bridget to step into the truth of who she is: she is not meant to be a doctor. Even though I feel this deep in my bones, how can I or anyone tell another person what they should or should not do? I remind myself that Bridget is asking for help in healing a medical problem for which she has found no relief. Expressing my insight is necessary, but first I need to do my best to relieve her seizures.

"Bridget, why don't you lie on the massage table, and we'll see if we can reduce some of the seizure activity." My hands have been aching to hold her head. The electrical impulses in her brain are screaming for attention.

I slip both of my hands under her head and begin scanning her brain. I'm looking for energetic imbalances and they're everywhere, disjointed pulses that look like multicolored strands of electricity, flying quickly all over the place.

"The light show in your brain is incredible. I'm not sure how you sleep at night."

"The sleep thing goes back and forth. Some nights I get no sleep, and other nights I get more than enough. I'm currently on the no-sleep plan. Since the seizures started, I have been exhausted and mentally slow."

I know intuitively that Bridget is a very creative person. The light in her brain, although currently disorganized, tells me that her true self is fun and artistic. A few times while watching the light show, I almost laugh out loud. The feelings confirm my insight that Bridget's personality is more that of an artist's or an actor's than a doctor's. I think that while physicians occasionally have creative moments, those times are limited. The brain I am looking at needs to express itself in an unlimited way.

* * *

SIXTH CHAKRA—TRUSTING YOUR INTUITION

The sixth chakra, or third eye, is located in the center of your brain. At its highest vibration, its color is a deep indigo. Emotionally, the sixth chakra is about feeling comfortable with and trusting your intuition. Intuition is not meant for just some people to use; it's meant for everyone. The sixth chakra governs the eyes, nose, ears, brain, hypothalamus, pituitary gland, and pineal gland. Through the awareness of the third eye, we can become multisensory beings. It is our birthright to see, feel, hear, and sense beyond our three-dimensional world and understand much more deeply our physical reality. As the sixth chakra spins, it energizes the brain and senses.

* * *

I can tell from looking at Bridget's mind that she is stubborn. I see sharp angles floating around in her brain that represent inflexibility. Even though her current circumstances make it impossible for her to continue attending medical school, she isn't ready to discover who she really is. I decide to have a conversation with her to introduce a career alternative to conventional medicine. I hope it won't shock her system. A career in medicine is certainly a logical choice for an intelligent, kindhearted person such as Bridget, but in all honesty, I feel it is not her life path.

"You have a very creative mind, Bridget; it's the mind of an artist. Have you ever thought that your talents might be best served in a more creative medical field, such as naturopathy?"

Bridget's body stiffens. Her muscles have contracted from her toes all the way up to her head, and my hands have felt the entire progression. Simultaneously, my vision notices a slow-ing of her energy. Somehow my words have created some sort of resistance. I know I'm on the right track because I've seen and felt this type of resistance after asking a question. Most people avoid what's uncomfortable, but the path to healing is generally found where we don't want to look.

"Funny, my seizures led me to you, to natural medicine, but professionally, it doesn't interest me."

Wow, thank goodness I haven't said what I was really seeing. Bridget's path has nothing to do with medicine. I work quietly balancing the energy in her brain for several minutes, watching her energy pick up speed, which relaxes her.

Bridget's relaxed state releases trapped energy in her brain, sending huge amounts of it into the room. I guide it out of my office with my mind, and happily notice a large energetic void in her head.

I gently rub Bridget's shoulder and ask, "Are you feeling cozy now?"

"Yes, I'm feeling better, thank you."

I try to focus on Bridget's words as she speaks, but I can hardly hear her. It's as if she's talking under water. Her brain, on the other hand, captures all my attention. I feel as if I've been transported into her cerebral cortex, surrounded by bil-lions of neurons firing thousands of synaptic connections, which look like fibers crisscrossing her head. It's stunningly beautiful. I shift my gaze to a place that draws me deep inside her brain. There is a lot of energy firing in this area, too. As I get closer, I see what looks like a fireworks display—mul-ticolored light jumps into a space. The space is cramped, making me feel that it's not a safe place for such a display. As I get closer, I hear noise that seems out of place—a loud popping mixed with an eerie sound, like metal rubbing on metal. It's disorienting. I realize the light show and sounds should not be here.

I begin moving healing energy at rapid pace into the spot. I wonder what will happen when the new energy mixes with the sound and light show in this small area. I know that all I need to do is run light—universal loving energy—into the areas that draw my attention and changes will occur. However, I generally have no real idea what will happen. Will Bridget's seizures stop today? Will they continue but decrease in intensity? Or will they remain unchanged? What I do know is that in our session, she's learning about herself, which causes her brain to realign. This learning, mostly unconscious, will impress upon Bridget what her soul wishes her to know.

Bridget leaves my office an hour and a half later. She won't return until next week. I pray that her seizures will subside between now and then, and I wish her beautiful health in every way.

• • •

How to Become a Multisensory Being

Using intuition is like having a vast internal encyclopedia that explains in extraordinary depth the meaning of events in your life and the world around you. Without it, we struggle with unnecessary pain and a lack of joy. Intuition expresses its meaning through color, light, sound, nature, taste, smell, the words of others, and, most importantly, through your feelings. Our intuition can perceive the future and heal the past because it provides a more accurate picture of unresolved problems. Its greatest significance, however, is to inform you about the best possible choice at any moment. To be intuitive means to see, hear, and feel clearly.

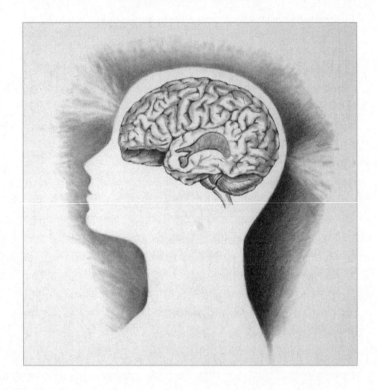

FIGURE 11. *The sixth chakra governs the brain—where neurotransmitters live. The hypothalamus and pituitary gland are shown here. The sixth chakra is often called the third eye and is located at the front and back of the head.*

Intuitive information enters the body through the back mate of the sixth chakra, located at the occipital ridge, the bump at the back of your head. Once the back mate receives intuitive information, it moves through your brain and into the front mate of the sixth chakra, which is located at your forehead. The role of the front mate is to translate intuitive information into language that makes sense to those of us living in a physical world. As we strengthen our intuition, it flows into every cell of our bodies, allowing us to be multisensory beings.

•   •   •

Bridget looks jovial as she walks through my office door a week later. Her doctor has kept me up to speed about her seizure activity; amazingly, it has decreased by 80 percent. I am thrilled and shocked to hear that her condition has dramatically changed after one session, but I am eager to hear Bridget herself tell me how she's doing.

"Thank you so much for your help, Marie," she says. "Things are improving!"

"I want to point out that each person heals themselves. I can facilitate healing, but you're really the one healing yourself. I can move energy in and out of your body, but what you choose to do with the energy, and the change it creates, is completely up to you."

"Are you saying that the healing has always been up to me?"

"Yes."

"So what was so different last week than all the previous weeks? Was it just the energy that created the change in me?"

"No, I believe that the intuitive feelings I sense when I work on others can ignite a significant change."

"You mean the subject that I don't want to talk about?"

"Yes. Why don't you hop on the table so we can continue our conversation?" I pat the table with my hand.

"How did you feel after your session last week?"

"Peaceful."

"Good. Did you take that as a sign?"

"I'm not sure what you mean."

"Bridget, I think the answers to life are simple. We humans make them more complicated than necessary."

"I still don't get your meaning. I'm sorry."

I stand at Bridget's left side, with my left hand resting on her heart chakra and my right hand resting on her left knee, in order to ground her in her body.

"Can we talk about medical school?"

"Yes, I know that's where you're heading."

"How do you know that I want to steer the conversation in that direction?"

"It was like the elephant in the room last week."

I chuckle, grateful that Bridget has a good sense of humor.

"I don't think it's a coincidence that your seizures came back with a vengeance while you were in medical school. And the fact that the seizures couldn't be treated with conventional medicine, which you were studying, is also a sign."

"So you think I need to pay attention to meaningless coincidences."

"Yes."

"But what about logic?"

"Logic is very important for us to navigate the earth. The logical part of our brains helps us get up on time in the morning, eat breakfast, put on clothing, and get to work. But when it comes to figuring out how to live a joyful life, the logical brain can't point us in the right direction. That's because we're often consumed by our logical thoughts, the majority of which are toxic. We might need to worry some about changing the oil in our car so it runs properly, but basing all of our decisions on our worries and doubts only creates fearful lives."

. . .

INTUITION AND THE BRAIN

We are all born intuitive. To be intuitive is a natural state of being. If your family and the community you grew up in recognized and supported your intuition, you would be using it today to guide your life. Unfortunately, most people don't recognize its importance and don't use it. Instead, many of us have been taught to make choices only with our minds. Your real feelings are your natural guidance system, and they don't reside in your brain.

Each of us is an individual who feels and experiences life in a way that's different from anyone else on the planet. Yet many of us have become lost doing what society says we should do. If we listened to our unique feelings, we would know what is perfect for us to do at any time. The best way to activate our intuition is to give our overworked brains a break. The brain requires very few energy particles to work well. Yet most people use huge amounts of energy in their brains by thinking, thinking, thinking. Then they process what they thought and then think some more. The brain is easily exhausted by our harried thoughts, always trying to decide between the lesser of two evils. Intuition does not view life in black-and-white terms the way the brain does. Intuition is gray, ever changing and evolving.

A Hundred Points of Energy

To work well and zip information around your central nervous system, the brain requires a lot of energy that comes from glucose, cholesterol, and Omega 3, 6, and 9. However, it needs fewer subatomic particles than the rest of your body because the brain conserves energy in comparison with other organs. The brain's true power is its ability to house valuable wisdom and insight meant to be available whenever you need it in order to creatively and calmly solve your life's various hiccups. Overanalyzing life through logic causes excessive energetic particles to accumulate in the brain, which actually tires it out in the same way your body reacts after eating too much sugar. In fact, the brain works ten times better with less life-force energy.

Imagine that each day you receive 100 points of energy for your whole body to utilize. The brain only needs 10 to 20 of these points to work extraordinarily well. The rest of your organs and body systems below the neck require 80 to 90 points of daily energy to maintain their health and well-being. When you spend too much time rationalizing, energy rushes to your brain. This decreases valuable space needed to store and share deep insight. Meanwhile the rest of your body will be starving for energy.

The best way to solve this inner dilemma is to practice being present. (Please see exercise on page 126.)

By repeatedly overusing our brain, we deplete the rest of our body of energy. We have many organs that require energy. Most of them reside below the neck, yet millions of people prevent energy from reaching them because their brains are using most of their energy.

Intuition is based on our personal feelings, not our thoughts. Getting out of the brain helps us be in the present moment while releasing pent-up energy into the rest of the body, energizing it.

I see people all day long who are asking for guidance to resolve problems. The information they seek is present within their being, but they can't use their intuition to find it because they're thinking too much. If they allow the third eye to receive psychic information, then they can translate the data into useable knowledge which will assist them in becoming who they really are. Intuition is like a muscle; if you don't use it, it atrophies.

* * *

Bridget is beginning to understand that she values logic and responsibility over personal happiness like most people in our society.

"So are you saying I need to use a perspective other than logic to figure out what's best for me?"

"Yes."

"I'm so used to using logic to analyze my life. How do I do what you're suggesting?"

"I can tell you're a very creative person, Bridget. The color and light in your brain looks like a piece of art. You also have a library there, a symbol I frequently see when a person is very intelligent. I often comment that such a person could be a physician. I can understand your confusion between smart and art. I think choosing both paths would totally fulfill you."

"Wow, you don't mince words."

"No, I figure by the time a client decides to see someone like me, they have tried many things to solve their problem, and their time is precious. So Bridget, tell me, what really brings you happiness?

Bridget wastes no time describing a summer program near Lake Tahoe where she worked. The program included writing workshops and improvisational acting. As she speaks, the program comes alive in my mind. Because of her enthusiastic joy, I feel as though I am there with her, reliving her experiences.

"Now that's what I'm talking about—what are you feeling in this moment?"

"Those were the best summers of my life. I miss camp and often think about it."

I can feel Bridget's sadness that those wonderful times are over.

"What you felt at that camp is called happiness. It's normal to do what you love and brings you joy."

"What about responsibility and acting like an adult?"

"Some people, Bridget, are delighted to work in the medical field. Forget about feeling responsible. Each of us has natural talents, which we discover through feeling bliss. Do you think one reason you remember those summers so well is because your happiness let you be in your body?"

"Yes, definitely."

"How would you feel if you were present in your body during class in medical school?"

"I knew that question was coming," Bridget says with a laugh. "I'm not sure. I'll have to sit with that a little while."

"OK, but why don't we try being present right now? Being in your body is the way to feel your intuition, and it's easy. It doesn't require endless mental processing, or talking it over with several friends to figure out what you want. You already know, and you have always known. The key to finding out is unlocking your innate ability to be present. Intuition speaks in the moment.

"I'd like you to close your eyes and feel your feet in your socks."

"OK," Bridget says, sounding skeptical.

"Great. Now feel, with the nerves beneath your skin, the weight and texture of your socks."

I see Bridget's brain become less heavy as a rush of energy quickly leaves her head and travels toward her toes.

"Wow, I can actually feel the fabric!"

I can see her mind growing more aware of the present. "Right now you're present with a part of yourself you normally ignore. Let's try an experiment with your newfound awareness: while maintaining the connection you now have with your feet, allow your mind to travel back to medical school, perhaps by imagining that you're sitting in a lab."

"I can do that."

"Good. Is it easy to imagine being there?"

"Surprisingly, yes. I feel like I'm really there."

"Good. Ask yourself, in this moment, if you're happy to be there. Then compare those feelings to how you felt while working those summers in Tahoe."

There's a pause while Bridget gets in touch with her memories. Finally she speaks. "At first I felt a little numb while I imagined sitting in class, but when you asked me to compare my feelings from the two different experiences, it became clear that in class I felt anxious, worried, and competitive—definitely not happy."

"You're doing this exercise very well, Bridget. Do you think the anxiety and other feelings played a role in the seizure activity?"

"Yes, I've learned a lot about stress and the body since all this happened."

"Do you think your dad lived a fairly stressful life?"

Bridget's energy changes, as I thought it would, when I direct the conversation toward her family and the underlying cause of her health problems. However, it doesn't explode into a massive perplexed ball, as I had feared. Instead, to my surprise, her energy stops. I know this is impossible, because Bridget's heart is still beating and she is breathing normally. Yet, from my inner perception, her energy is frozen.

My solid-energy vision reminds me of an illustration sketched with dark shades of charcoal. The particles that I normally see moving throughout the body now resemble tiny rocks. Nothing is moving.

"Why did you ask about my father?" The sound of Bridget's voice abruptly ends my fascination with what I am seeing.

"When we first met, your father's energy shared information with me about the stress you're under. I think your father wants you to avoid some of the choices he made, so your life can be different."

Bridget looks up with a start. I can see her stationary energy start to free itself. "What do you mean, my dad is trying to help me?"

"I use intuition to understand many things, even those beyond this world. Your father's energy tells me that he worked very hard and didn't spend as much time with his family as he would have liked. He wishes he had allowed himself more freedom."

Bridget begins to cry softly. "When did you know this about my dad?"

"The day we met. Your father has always been proud of you. He may have pushed you too hard at times, and you easily surpassed his expectations. But now he understands more than ever how precious our time is here."

My hands cradle Bridget's head. She reaches up to hold my left arm and says, "Thank you."

A week later, Bridget returns, still looking peaceful, but with a new hairdo.

"I love your new do," I say when she enters the office. Bridget had shaved her head.

She laughs. "Thank you. I decided I needed to start all over again and find me, apart from all the things I think are me."

"That's very profound, Bridget. It takes a lot of courage to strip away who you think you are so you can become who you *truly* are."

"Marie, our session last week was life-altering. I don't know if you actually spoke with my dad or how you know what you know, but your words were exactly what I needed to hear, and I can still feel their effects all through my body. Now that the seizures are no longer paralyzing me, I've decided to put off medical school a little longer and spend time getting to know myself."

I continued to see Bridget regularly for one year. She decided not to return to medical school, and went on to become a writer and actor. She resides in the Seattle area and works as a web content editor. She also teaches writing workshops, is a songwriter, and performs and produces her own one-woman shows. She remains seizure-free.

* * *

Exercises for the Sixth Chakra

The following exercises are for the sixth chakra and all the organs and systems it governs. They will help you learn how to connect to your intuition and strengthen its incredible muscle.

One-Minute Recharge
This quick exercise will energetically strengthen the sixth chakra.

1. Sit down.
2. While keeping your head still, make large circles with your eyes in a clockwise direction for fifteen seconds.
3. Change direction, moving your eyes in large counterclockwise circles for fifteen seconds.
4. Look up at the ceiling and down to the floor for another fifteen seconds.
5. Look as far as you can to the left and then to the right for fifteen seconds.

Becoming Present
To begin the process of being present, allow your mind to let your nerves physically feel the clothing that is touching your skin. Perhaps feel your socks on your feet. As you become present with your socks and the skin touching them, ask yourself: What is my skin feeling? Are the socks tight, loose, or heavy? Is the fabric of my socks cotton, synthetic, or both? (Reminder: don't let your brain answer this question!) Practice becoming aware of your physical body in the moment multiple times a day for about thirty seconds. Being present heightens awareness—enabling us to make better choices—and energizes the body.

Journal about Your Intuition
To realize that *you already know what is best for you* is a positive step toward trusting your intuition. Keeping an extrasensory journal (making notes of your abilities beyond normal senses) helps you develop an understanding of your

own unique perception. Following are simple steps to assist you on your extrasensory journal adventure:

1. Write either first thing in the morning or later in the evening, when you can have quiet time away from the chores of daily life.

2. Choose a comfortable place to sit and clear your mind. Take a few moments and breathe deeply to relax. (You can also use the Grounding through Visualization exercise on page 24.)

3. Once your mind is peaceful, close your eyes and say a few kind words to yourself. Self-appreciation attracts energy, allowing more information to become available as you write.

4. You will need to be in your body as much as possible when you write. Feel your feet, your socks, or your bottom where you're sitting.

5. When writing, include hunches, feelings, or visions if they arise. Pay attention to how your body feels, too, and make a note of it.

6. Now that you're relaxed and centered, your first task is to simply ask yourself questions. Write each question at the top of a clean page in your journal. The questions can be specific: which college would be best for my child to attend next year? Or they can be general: what is the most important thing I need to know at this moment? If you're not sure what to ask, here are several suggestions:

   - How am I doing at balancing my life?
   - Is there anything I need to know about my family right now?
   - What areas of work are best suited for me?

- How is my health?
- What is the best advice I could give a family member at this time?
- What is the most important thing I need to know about (fill in the blank) _____ at this time?

7. After asking a question, return to an awareness of your body and feeling relaxed. Real answers come when we are calm.

8. Write down whatever comes to you. Include full sentences, visions, feelings in your body, and colors or words flashing across your mind or sounds you may be hearing.

9. Intuitively journal for no more than fifteen to twenty minutes at a time.

10. Once you have finished writing, put down your journal and walk away from it for a few minutes. This will allow some distance between receiving information and translating it into something meaningful.

11. When you return to your journal and read what you wrote, ask yourself, "What I am feeling as I read each word?" Pay attention to the answers that make you feel curious. It's through curiosity that we open up to authentic knowledge and the multisensory being that each of us is.

12. If you feel fear during this exercise, it's most likely that your mind is overthinking and trying to process the answers. Fear is rarely a sign of intuition. Practice getting out of your head and feeling rather than thinking.

13. It's very possible that on your first try, you will understand the answers to your question and marvel

at how intuitive you are! If you don't, please don't worry; the meaning of your answers will become clear. Many times when I do this exercise, I may not know initially what the answers mean, but because I feel curiosity about them, I know their meaning has value, and in time I will discover what that is.

14. Be patient; a common turnaround time for answers could be three days or longer.

15. Most likely you will receive complete understanding of your answers when you least expect it, usually in the form of an "aha" moment. If you do, go back to your journal and reread your answers. This time they will make more sense and will validate your abilities, helping them to grow.

Children are naturally multisensory, but may begin to forget this innate ability near age seven due to our overly structured educational system. If your children are younger than seven, encourage natural curiosity and a connection to the unseen world. If they are older, remind them of the insight they expressed when younger. The reminder will automatically connect them to their amazing senses.

Here is a helpful tool to reinforce intuition no matter their age. You will need five envelopes and five different pictures of solid colors. Place one color into each envelope and close it. Have your children hold each closed envelope one at a time, and ask them to use their senses to gather information about the color inside. Color is personal and can affect each of us differently. Ask your children how they feel about each envelope and pay attention to their intuitive expression of each color. Your children's descriptions are helpful insights into how they experience intuition.

Visualization: Expand the Third Eye

The front of the sixth chakra is meant to extend out of the head. When it does, it's capable of translating intuitive information, such as metaphors, pictures, and feelings into meanings. Try this simple visualization to extend your third eye.

1. Stand three feet away from a blank wall or door. You can keep your eyes open or closed.
2. Now visualize a white tunnel in the wall. The tunnel is cone-shaped and is narrower at the end farthest from you. It extends about three feet into the wall.
3. Now imagine that the tunnel is spinning clockwise.
4. Now imagine that a two-inch version of yourself is standing in the tunnel, but you are not spinning.

Do this exercise for several minutes a day until you notice your world becoming more vibrant because you have expanded your third eye.

— 8 —

Seventh Chakra

Connecting to Spirit

STEPHANIE CASUALLY STEPS INTO MY office, a place she has visited many times, though never to see me for a private session. She has shoulder-length blond hair, and her smile literally graces the room with light. In her thirties with an advanced degree in psychology, she is a therapist with a private practice. Six months ago, Stephanie joined my mentoring program, a year-long process in which students deepen their understanding of energy medicine. I am curious. Why did she make an appointment now? What could she possibly need that she isn't getting out of the mentoring program?

I first met Stephanie one and a half years ago at one of my Reiki workshops. I was instantly drawn to her; our energy systems resonated with each other as if we were old buddies. I soon realized that she is very intuitive. Stephanie has a great desire to utilize her intuitive talents as an energy medicine professional and do less work as a therapist.

Today I'm amazed again at how comfortable I am with her. For just a moment, I wonder if she'd like to skip her session and go out for drinks and a chat.

After lying down on the massage table, Stephanie says, "I'm embarrassed to tell you what's been happening. But that's why I scheduled a private session with you."

I scan her body several times in a matter of seconds. Nothing unusual pops into my perception. What can she possibly be embarrassed about? She's not having affairs, telling lies, or cheating in any other way. Just as I begin to pull out of my scan, her body tells me, so fast I almost miss it, that she's cheating herself.

Scanning is a way to receive information about a person's body even before they tell me their symptoms or as they are explaining them. In this way I can track what's really going on in their body as they're talking, because the body always knows. Many times the clients who make appointments to see me have already seen several health practitioners, including conventional doctors who were unable to diagnose or successfully treat them. This is frustrating to the client who is tired of their symptoms and even more tired of worrying that something is seriously wrong, yet undiscovered. Scanning for me begins as an auditory experience. I literally listen to the body. My ears take the whole body in its awareness as a single unit. For some reason bodies know that I can hear them so they generally talk up a storm when I'm working with them or sometimes even when I'm standing next to a stranger while waiting in line at my local coffee shop.

When sounds are expressed as language or when I detect odd sounds coming from the body, I then direct my attention to the energy and anatomy in the area, which I can energetically visualize with my mind. In Stephanie's case, as she spoke I listened to hear if her body was agreeing with her words.

I'm always astonished by how the body knows when it's being scanned and so communicates what it needs.

A Quick Energetic Scan
to Charge Your Energy System

In the last chapter of this book, you will find a detailed explanation about how you can scan your energy system. Sometimes we don't have the time to spend doing a comprehensive scan so here is an example of a quick one!

You will want to find a comfortable place to stand with plenty of room around you, approximately three feet in each direction. With your hands at your side begin moving them up slowly—about one minute per inch. Your goal is to get your hands to come together above your head. As you move your hands slowly upward, you will want to imagine your chakra system. This scan will help you become familiar with your chakras and charge your energy system at the same time.

In your mind's eye, imagine your first chakra, a beautiful red cone about one foot in length spinning in between your legs. Let your imagination feel its velocity and the strength of its color.

As your being becomes conscious of the chakra's energy, your imagination will charge the vortexes with life-sustaining energy and help them release any stagnation.

As you scan, keep your hands slowly moving up to assist you in charging your chakras and visualizing their advancement.

Good job! Now move your attention up to the second chakra. It is amazingly orange and vibrant with life. Feel its energy in the abdomen and at your lower back.

Wonderful! Now move on to the third chakra. Feel how much it loves your immune system. It is yellow like the sun and powerful beyond measure.

Now focus on the fourth chakra and its vibrant green color. Move your hands closer to the heart center, steep your mind with love—love for this moment, love for you, and all that exists.

You may feel your energy quicken as you enter the higher vibrational chakra territory. Take a few deep breaths and relax into your incredible energy.

Fabulous! Now feel the fifth chakra and its ability to empower you. Imagine its blue color of truth as it spins at your neck.

Fantastic! Now move to your sixth chakra and see beyond this world. Imagine its deep color of indigo.

Amazing! You are doing a great job charging your energy and getting to know your chakra system.

Now with your hands above your head imagine the incredible light coming from this vortex. Its bright white light can reach far into the heavens. With your hands together, send energy past your body into your aura, and let your aura come alive with your awareness—as if your aura were water, pure, and calming. Let your being enjoy a few moments of this exchange.

You can do this scan any time you wish in order to charge your energy system. You might want to do it with your eyes closed to enhance your imagination. Enjoy!

"Stephanie, whatever you share with me today will not leave this room."

"I know," she says nervously, nodding her head. Her eyes tear up as she describes her concern. "My mom is literally nuts."

I smile jokingly.

"No, I'm not kidding. She's crazy. One of the things I worry about most is becoming like her."

The smile falls from my face and I show her my genuine concern.

"My mother's madness is one reason why I became a therapist. On top of her being dysfunctional, she's a hypochondriac. I'm afraid I'm a hypochondriac, too."

Without thinking, I am drawn to Stephanie's right shoulder and physically soothe the area. She takes a deep breath, sheds a few tears, and then quickly wipes them away.

"OK, I see that any hint that you're like your mother upsets you, but I'm sure there are great things about your mom, and those are the only qualities that are truly inside you."

Stephanie tilts her head slightly and stares at me, as if to say *I hope to God you're right.*

"Why don't we start with you explaining your symptoms and see where they lead us?"

She wipes more tears from her face and tries to relax. I'm drawn to the top of her head, the crown where the seventh chakra sits, and I gently rest my hands there.

"So, tell me all about it."

Stephanie places one hand on her right clavicle, just below her shoulder. "My most recent symptom began a month ago. There's a lump of some kind right here, and it hurts. I have pain on and off in different areas of my body, odd symptoms like tingling, swelling, and numbness. I have gone to see doctors over the years, and I get embarrassed because they never find anything."

"Did you see your doctor about this most recent lump?"

"Yes, I finally went yesterday. He thinks it's nothing to worry about but wants me to get an X-ray to be sure."

"Good. I believe nothing will show up on the X-ray, but I can see why you have frequently tried to have your symptoms diagnosed. During my most recent energetic scan of your body, I noticed your seventh chakra is misfiring, which can affect your peripheral neurological system. I can literally see sparks and ash coming off your seventh chakra."

· · ·

Seventh Chakra — You Are Spirit

The seventh chakra, or crown chakra, is located on top of the head and governs the skin and the peripheral nervous system (the nerves outside of the brain and spinal column). It is white in color, and one of the three chakras that extend visually outside of the body. Emotionally, this chakra is about individuating through recognizing your connection to spirit. Spirit can be anything: a tree, a flower, or something larger and more powerful than one can imagine, like the universe. For me, spirit is pure energy. For others, it's God. How and whom or what you identify with doesn't matter. What does matter is becoming aware that you are an extraordinary, irreplaceable part of spirit.

This particular chakra pulls energy into the body from outside of the earth atmosphere—what we metaphorically think of as the heavens. When this chakra is out of balance, people generally experience peripheral neurological symptoms, such as tingling, pain, numbness, or other odd and

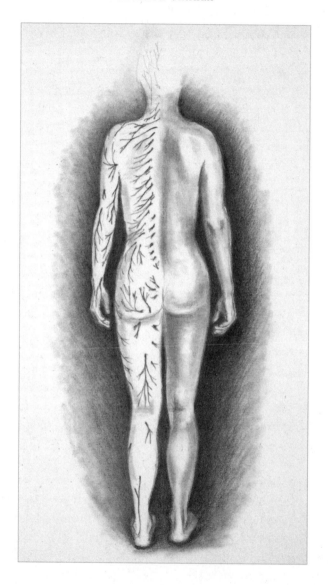

FIGURE 12. *The peripheral nervous system on the left and the skin on the right are two of the many ways we connect to spirit.*

somewhat challenging symptoms to diagnose. These symptoms can be felt anywhere on the body.

One way to stabilize the seventh chakra is to activate the smaller chakras at the bottom of each foot and pull up earth energy. When the body receives energy from the earth, it can better balance the seventh chakra because the first chakra is the mate to the seventh. As we grow spiritually, we must be rooted deeply to the earth.

INDIVIDUATION

Although we are all part of one spirit, we are also individual beings of light. Each of us is a singular illumination in the universe, humming a specific energy that no one else can. Many people have a hard time recognizing and believing in their specialness. Many are afraid to shine their unique light into the world and to be seen as incredible human beings. Instead, many of us want to conform—to look alike, talk alike, think alike—in short, to appear normal. When we go through the process of individuating, we naturally gain access to our genius, a place we hardly know exists, hidden as it is from our consciousness. We hide these doorways into our brilliance because we are afraid of our true power and innate gifts.

All of us live here on Earth to engage our soul so that we may know love and ultimately *be* love. As such, we are incredibly gifted. Our talents, which we each possess, have been crafted with pure, passionate love. Your job while you journey on Earth is to discover your beautiful, unusual self and live your life out loud—not only to bring lasting joy into your life but to share the energy of feeling whole with the rest of the universe so that we may all live in unimaginably positive ways.

You are always connected to the Divine. Finding ways to experience your constant connection can give you confidence to move forward in life and embrace all that you are.

* * *

I reconnect to Stephanie's feet with my mind to encourage her body to ground, hoping the misfiring in her seventh chakra will reduce.

Stephanie's muscles tighten as her anxiety level quickly climbs. As a mentoring student, she knows why her seventh chakra is misfiring, but having knowledge doesn't guarantee an easy transition into healing.

"Stephanie, you have always been aware of your intuitive capabilities," I tell her. "As a child, you were wiser than most of your family members. Your parents couldn't have accepted your uniqueness, so you hid it because you wanted to be loved."

Stephanie's energy suddenly becomes feisty. As always, I'm happy to receive such clear communication. I'm now intrigued about the meaning of these assertive feelings.

"My childhood was a seriously crazy set of circumstances," she says. "I had to fight against the senselessness to maintain stability and successfully leave home. My mother lied and was manipulative and I never felt any real structure in my home. I worry that the events in my childhood may have an effect on my relationships with my husband and children. Most of the time I believe I am a sane and balanced person, but when my undiagnosed physical symptoms resurface, I start to compare myself to my mother."

Clearly Stephanie's feelings are strong, and I'm sure they're justified. Despite her tendency to assert her fury when her family is mentioned, I can tell she's worked hard to heal her childhood wounds. I can't see the effect of any damaging family behaviors in her root chakra. But for some reason, the therapeutic healing she's done to date has not integrated at the cellular level. Her mind has gotten the message about her life now, but for some reason the rest of the cells in her body didn't get the memo and are creating confusion within her peripheral nervous system.

"Stephanie, I admire the effort you've made to be your own person and not be affected by your family's negative patterns. You have successfully educated yourself and created a lovely and healthy family of your own. I think you can stop fighting against what happened years ago because it no longer exists."

Tears run down Stephanie's face. She doesn't bother to wipe them away.

"I can hear you. And I understand what you said, but my body can't seem to stop fighting."

"Stephanie, you're safe. Your mother is in your life only when you want her to be, right?"

"Right," she says with little enthusiasm.

I lower my head closer to Stephanie's midsection and close my eyes to visualize the nerves throughout her body. Within a few moments, hundreds of tiny white lights begin flashing all over her body, indicating nerve activity. I direct calming energy into her peripheral nervous system while repeating silently, "You are safe." I also tell her nerves about Stephanie's current life so that they will accurately update her cells, allowing them to react from truth rather than her history.

"Whatever you're doing feels so good," Stephanie says. "Please don't stop."

"Of course!" I say, while maintaining a telepathic conversation with her nerves telling them they are safe.

After a while I begin a second conversation with Stephanie to help her integrate her innate intuitive abilities. She's hidden them from the rest of the world because she didn't want to appear unbalanced due to her childhood.

"Stephanie, do you tell people about your intuition?"

"No."

There is a long pause, but I sense that she has more to say. I wait.

"I don't trust it, but it's been easier to consider its importance since joining the mentoring group."

"I'm happy to hear that. What do you think will need to happen for you to embrace this part of your unique connection to creation?"

"I'm not sure; I have just begun to consider that very question."

"Have you considered that you don't have to do a thing to receive unconditional love from the heavens? Receiving is a passive experience. Feeling, even for just a few moments, a sense of worthiness is all you need."

"Yes, I remember that from our mentoring group. But receiving that kind of love is actually hard work. I have to get out of my head and stop the self-limiting dialogue that tells me I'm not good enough to receive it."

"You're not unique in limiting yourself, Stephanie. You are unique in your awareness of your negative voices and how they hold you back. Everyone is unique, and everyone has a gift. Some might be gifted physically, musically, or intellectually, and others might have a special insight. What I find most amazing about our talents is that once we discover and express them, more follow. In other words, gifts beget gifts. Letting fear trap you into not offering your gift one that you have known about for years—prevents you from enjoying all those other gifts you have to impart to others."

Stephanie tilts her head up at me. "Are you saying I'm holding back more than my intuition?"

"Yes. There is always more to understand, appreciate, and perceive about ourselves. We are not just one thing. After you discover something about yourself, there will always be more to discover. It's like children learning how to walk. Once they start walking, they start learning how to run."

"I'm a little overwhelmed by what you're saying. I'm afraid to be all I can be, and now you're telling me that there is so much more."

"What are you afraid of?" I scan her energy system as I ask; I want to find the source of her fear and where it is constricting her body. A large swirl of green and blue energy gathers at her solar plexus, like a storm threatening to break.

At the same time, I notice that Stephanie's seventh chakra begins to close down. The large cone splits in several pieces, into what looks like the petals of a flower. One petal folds down, closing the place where the seventh chakra enters her body. Stephanie suddenly feels cold to me, and I place a warm blanket on her. Energy can change quickly as thoughts and feelings change. If her body cools down, more energetic constriction will follow.

"Stephanie, if you open to spirit, you will receive the guidance needed to be less fearful of who you are and whatever disease you may or may not have. If you continue to misfire and close your seventh chakra, your fear will continue to stifle your life."

• • •

OPENING TO THE SPIRIT IN EVERYTHING

In the eyes, ears, and arms of the universe, you are perfect—no matter who you are, what you do, or what you have or haven't accomplished. The universal spirit cherishes even the most hardened criminal. If human beings could feel for a moment this authentic, magical, unconditional love, our individual and collective lives would completely change.

Spirituality is the journey of one's soul learning how to unite with divinity. Connecting to spirit is an individual experience. When you connect, your being soars in ecstasy.

Spirit is what sings to your heart, and spirit is nothing. Spirit can show up as a feather, a child's tear, or a single wave on the vast oceans. Where spirit shows up can be a complete surprise. Recently, NASA scientists decided to point the Hubble telescope at an area near the Milky Way where no stars were visible. The telescope took pictures for eleven days. When the film was developed, the scientists were shocked to see images of over 300,000 stars—proving once again that there is always something in what appears to be nothing.

Spirit could be mixed in with the lint in the front pocket of your jeans. It's probably talking to you right now, saying, "You are more than any star could be; you are beyond the beyond, and nothing will ever change that."

Listening, feeling, or having a relationship with spirit is always your choice. You may have felt your soul merge with spirit when you held your child for the first time, saw a gorgeous sunset, or hiked to an ocean overlook. The separateness you feel while living here on Earth is pure illusion. You are always connected to the Divine.

The first step is to recognize all the many ways that you hold yourself back from spirit. Then you'll know when you're feeling disconnected and immediately start reaching

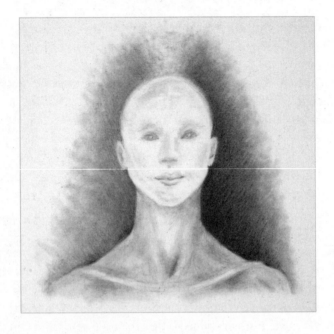

FIGURE 13. *The seventh chakra, which is located at the crown of the head, connects us to the universal spirit.*

for connection. When you identify feeling disconnected as separate from a normal everyday feeling and recognize that it doesn't serve your highest interest, you will be drawn to connecting because of how it enhances your life.

• • •

"Stephanie, let's try this new technique, OK?"

"Sure."

"When your body does weird things that frighten you, similar to the pain near your clavicle, this means you are disconnected from source energy. Can you find a place in your body right now that is uncomfortable?"

Stephanie looks a little puzzled, pulling her eyebrows together and scrunching up her forehead.

"Actually, during the last five minutes I have been a little nauseous."

"I'm sorry to hear that, but good, your body has conditioned itself to disconnect. It repeats this pattern as often as it can. Would it be hard to become aware of another part of your body that is working just fine?"

"You mean stop thinking about the nausea and start thinking about some place in my body that is at peace?"

"Exactly."

"I think that would be very hard."

"Great."

Stephanie laughs out loud but also sounds annoyed. "I don't get you, Marie. Why would you say 'great' when what you're asking would be hard for me?"

Regardless of Stephanie's struggle, she is clearly ready to let go of things that no longer work for her. I can sense her energy system throughout her body maintaining a steady, peaceful flow.

"Change is rarely easy. Your resistance to my suggestion is a sign that we're on the right track. No one wants to let go of their defense mechanisms, but eventually we realize that making positive changes means doing what's unfamiliar."

• • •

RESISTANCE

The only thing that keeps us from moving forward in our lives is fear. While in a fearful state, generally in childhood, we create defense mechanisms. Defense mechanisms are behaviors that distance us from being fully aware of unpleasant thoughts, feelings, and actions. When our defense systems were created, they may have served a purpose. But over time, as we mature, they become a force that resists flow. Many times we resist releasing old, outdated defenses, even though they are unhealthy, because their familiarity provides a limited sense of comfort. That comfort is an illusion.

Turning against false protection ignites every alarm in the human body. The mind will do everything it can to protect itself from fear. But fear, too, is an illusion. My simple, positive suggestion to Stephanie wouldn't have been all that difficult or dangerous for her to carry out, but she immediately resisted it.

When we're fearful, even if there's no real danger, our mind reacts as if there were, creating chemical reactions that put our bodies into a fight-or-flight mode. Fortunately, outrunning an attacker or swerving to avoid a car accident are not everyday occurrences. Yet scary events happen in some people's minds and body chemistry many times a day, making it impossible for them to connect to spirit. I believe we have journeyed to Earth many times, so what are we really afraid of?

• • •

I begin to sense that Stephanie's energy system is shifting. She's starting to understand what her undiagnosed symptoms really mean.

"So worrying about the swelling near my right clavicle is a defense mechanism that's keeping me from being whole and expressing my true self. Is that right?"

"Yes, the answers to life are simple. And in your case, the answers won't be frequently found in your doctor's office. Connecting to the wisdom inside of you will calm your peripheral nervous system and lead you back to your truth—that you are a very intuitive person. You know."

Stephanie exhales deeply.

"When you hear truth, your being relaxes and the energy in your body runs smoothly, creating a stronger connection to your seventh chakra and spirit. Real truth comes from a healthy connection to spirit, not from fear and resistance. If you start to feel yourself going down the familiar road of fear, become curious."

My hands are on Stephanie's third chakra. She is so relaxed. I know she wants to ask me another question, but fortunately she is letting go and fully accepting her body moving at ease. Her third chakra is communicating to her seventh chakra. As I feel the magical interaction between chakras, a golden light resembling a laser beam appears between the third and seventh chakra. The light serves as a pathway, sending love and information back and forth. When the body is truly calm, the communion between chakras is profound.

Stephanie's third chakra is sending energy of appreciation to her seventh chakra for connecting to source energy. While observing their connection, I'm reminded of how the endocrine system communicates to all the organs in the body through the release of hormones. As I marvel at the amazing relationship between all things in the body, I also perceive that imbalances in Stephanie's seventh chakra have drastically slowed down her metabolic rate. If she can regularly return to this calm place of rest, her metabolic rate will jump-start itself, which will allow her to release unnecessary toxins from her body.

After a few minutes, Stephanie opens her eyes and asks, "Was there some sort of conversation going on in my body just now?"

I nod yes, appreciating her intuitive skills, and tell her what I heard.

"How can I keep the conversation going with all my chakras?"

"Become curious about your body, Stephanie, and new worlds will open up to you," I tell her. "Real human curiosity extends beyond space and time, making what we once perceived as a phenomenon, valid. We live in an ever-changing universe where every day, new discoveries expose our minds to great things that at first might seem odd. None of us knows for certain the real answers to life. Yet if we wonder instead of fear, hidden knowledge and events will be revealed."

Stephanie left my office that day more determined to connect to the magic in her life. She worked hard to recognize her resistances and move through them. She recently told me that now, when she experiences something not quite right in her body, she becomes curious and deepens her awareness of it, and the symptoms almost always lessen or disappear. Stephanie is working on expanding her private practice to include energy work and intuitive counseling so she may help others reach their connection with ease.

EXERCISES FOR THE SEVENTH CHAKRA
The following exercises are for the seventh chakra and all the organs and systems it governs. They will help you learn how to connect to spirit and your divine resources.

One-Minute Feeling Unconditional Love
This quick exercise will help you receive unconditional love from the heavens.

1. Gently tap on the top of your head using all ten fingers.
2. Then close your eyes and imagine warm light flooding into the top of your head.
3. After a moment or two, think of something or someone you really, really love.
4. Imagine the love you have for this person or thing mixing with the warm light.
5. Now think of yourself, and transform the love you have for this person or thing into love for yourself.

•

Like all of us, the spirit world is where your children came from before deciding to live a life on Earth. Their connection to this alternate dimension is valuable and can be enhanced to assist them in every area of their life now and in adulthood. Use the following exercise to maintain their connection to spirit.

Ask your child to draw a picture of a world they don't currently live in. Suggest that this world may be familiar or remind them of a magical place they visit when sleeping. Encourage conversation about the details of the drawing in order to pull out their knowledge of other realms, dimensions, and helpful beings.

Visualization: Realize Your Self-Worth

1. Sit in a comfortable place and close your eyes.
2. Take several deep breaths and, as you exhale, release any stress you might feel from your day.
3. Inhale peace and calm.

4. Breathe like this for at least three minutes.
5. When you notice that your body is at ease, imagine that you are at a party.
6. This party is in some far-off place in the cosmos. You do not need to know where or what the cosmos is.
7. Become curious and look around. Let your mind perceive other realms.
8. Visualize that every person, angel, or being for whom you have great regard is attending your party. Perhaps Martin Luther King, Jr., Gandhi, Jesus, Gaia, Buddha, Mary, the Archangel Michael, or someone else you would love to meet someday is there.
9. Notice that all of these exceptional beings treat you as an equal. They have the same regard for you as you do for them. Each person is excited to see you and embraces you. Everyone sees your beauty, gifts, and wholeness. Stay at the party for as long as you can, and absorb the love and light of your peers.

Seventh Chakra Connection to Spirit

Here is one of my favorite affirmations. Repeat it daily to assist you in feeling your connection to spirit.

In this world and all others,
I know that I'm cherished beyond measure.

Within this bright light of awareness,
I allow my natural gifts to rise into my consciousness,
and provide healing to myself and all beings
throughout the universes.

— 9 —

Scanning the Body
and the Human Aura

IT'S PERFECTLY NATURAL TO CREATE a healing relationship
with your body. One of the best ways to do so is through
fostering a knowledge of your health by visiting and sensing your energy centers. In this chapter I will explain step
by step how to perform a detailed scan of your body's
energy, organs, emotions, spiritual connections, and overall mental state.

Developing this type of rapport with yourself helps you
identify when you might require preventive treatment or
medical advice, or other forms of healing therapies. Listening
to your body also makes health-care decisions easier because
your body knows what's best for it. And as you get more
acquainted with your physical being, you will be able to read
important messages that guide you in living a healthy life.

The first important step is to map where your chakras are on
your body. You may want to scan your body in private as you
spend time getting to know their location. You will be placing
your non-dominant hand where you believe the chakra is, or in
some close proximity, getting acquainted for five to ten minutes
at each position. If you need a refresher as to the color, function,
and location of your chakras, see the chart in the appendix.

I recommend having a journal and a pen nearby so that you can record your findings with your dominant hand. Many times the experiences we have when we deeply connect to ourselves are very moving and in our excitement we might forget information coming into our awareness.

If you take your time when hanging out with your energy system, you will actually be spending more meaningful time with yourself. Research shows that solitude fosters peace of mind, a relaxed body, increased energy, heightened awareness, self-confidence, and increased enthusiasm and creativity.

As you scan your body, you will also send healing light as a preventive or to create any necessary positive change your body needs.

Choose the first chakra you wish to acquaint yourself with or start with chakra number one and move upward through the other chakras. It might be nice to gauge your energy system by moving through the chakras in order, as the three lower chakras are primal and vibrate at a lower frequency than chakras five, six, and seven. Chakra four, in the center of your chest, is the mid-heaven of your chakra system, where the capacity for energy begins to change (as described in chapter 4).

Before you begin, close your eyes and imagine where each vortex is in your body and how it might be feeling. Many times first impressions are correct. Also, remember if you feel fearful when you're imagining your chakras, that fear has nothing to do with intuition. Do your best to be kind to yourself when negative thoughts occur and bypass them with confidence.

When you're ready, rub your hands together rather quickly to stimulate the chakra in the center of each palm of your hands. These medium-sized chakras will gather insightful information about your energetic system and, as they spin, they will feed energy into your body, because like all chakras they receive and transmit life-force energy.

As you rub your hands together, imagine that the mid-sized vortex in each hand obtains data from your body—from the chakras, of course, but also from the organs and body systems that the chakras govern. For example, when your hand is on your solar plexus, or the third chakra, you could receive information about your endocrine system because the third chakra governs this part of the body.

I asked you to imagine information coming into your awareness through the chakras in your hands, because intention is very powerful. Let's add one more objective. Imagine and emotionally *feel* that your body is well, regardless of whether you have previously or are currently experiencing any health issues. Holding a positive thought accompanied with upbeat emotions charges your body with powerful healing energy.

Your body works very hard for you every day to maintain wellness, and on an energetic level you are well. Even if you're encountering a debilitating disease right now, you have a complete set of organs, bones, blood cells, and other body processes functioning perfectly as a hologram in the first layer of your auric field.

The First Auric Layer

The human aura surrounds the body like an eggshell and extends approximately seven feet away from it. The aura is divided into seven layers of different energy. The first layer of the field is the closest one to the body and begins about three inches away from your human form. It is organized with grid lines—stunningly beautiful beams of light that crisscross this auric field—and is considered a support for the other six fields. Within its energy field exists a hologram vibrating a replica of your internal workings in complete and total health. Its main job is to remind your physical body what health looks like. It does this best when it receives earth energy from the first chakra. This field may look grey-blue and somewhat fuzzy around the body. When I experience this field, I see organs, cells, and other body functions floating within its mass.

Now that you know some information about the first layer of your aura, it's nice to offer a prayer of gratitude for its constant healthy vibration maintaining your well-being each and every day. You can derive your own prayer or use the following:

Thank you dear aura for my amazing energetic system and its faithful and persistent pulsation, which brings amazing health into my being.

To watch a guided exercise on becoming aware of your auric field, visit SoundsTrue.com/bonus/ IntuitiveHealing

Great, now we're ready to move forward in making the first scan of your being. Do your best not to judge the information—only allow it to flow into your perception and trust that what you truly need will become available to you in its own perfect way.

Starting at the first chakra, rest your non-dominant hand just above the perineum (in front of you at the pelvic floor). Take a few minutes to get comfortable, and then ask a few questions. (Some examples follow.) Keep in mind that all answers are valuable even if they don't make sense in the moment. Your perception could be leading you, in its own flawless way, towards a deeper knowing.

1. How do I recognize this chakra? Is it shaped like an orb or cone for me? Or am I experiencing it as some other representation? Is there a color that pops into my mind, and if so, what is it? Are there any sounds that I'm experiencing while I'm concentrating here? If so, what are they and do they remind me of anything? If I were to gauge the size/length of this chakra, how do I sense it? Am I grounded? Do I feel or sense energetic vines or roots growing into the ground from my feet and am I returning earth energy to my body?

   Once you receive answers about the general function of your first chakra, write them down, or take a mental note of the information, then move on to asking about your emotions.

2. When I'm visiting my first chakra, are there any childhood emotions that come up for me? Have my childhood memories changed over the last five years? And if so, what stories have changed and healed? What insights have I gained about those who raised me? Am I able to see, feel, and hear clearly into the beginning of this lifetime? What areas feel gray and difficult?

As your intuition is studying your first chakra, also let your energy feel this chakra's connection to its mate, the seventh chakra. In your awareness of it, you can feel the earth and the heavens because you are both physical and light. How does it feel to embody both?

Again, take note of your findings. When you're ready, you can assess the physical function of your being that is in the hologram of the first layer of your aura.

Now, rub your hands together again for about one minute to recharge the chakras in them and to wash away any stagnant energy that they might have absorbed. The stagnant energy will be released into the universe and be recycled into vibrant energy. When you're ready, place your non-dominant hand close to your body—about three inches away—and feel your aura there. You may think you're rubbing the air. That's OK, because whether you see, hear, or feel it, allow yourself to know that it's there. Feel free to close your eyes to better feel your aura at any time. Sometimes blocking out the physical world by closing your eyes allows us to detach from reality so that we can really zone into our energy.

How are you sensing this layer of energy? Does a color appear in your mind or a particular feeling? Feelings are your natural guidance system, so if you're feeling at peace as you access this field, then that feeling could indicate that your body is healthy. If, on the other hand, you're feeling anxious, it could mean that your body is stressed. Stress is the leading cause of disease. If you're seeing a color, it could be in relationship to a particular chakra in the body. Or if you identify well with what colors express, then allow your previous connection to colors give you information. For example, let's say you love the color blue, and as you scan this part of your aura, a beautiful blue ocean appears in your mind, giving you waves of peace. This could be your being telling you how thrilled it is that you're connecting to your body more sincerely. Or that peace is yours even physically. Maybe you're hearing words or full sentences. Even if you think your mind is talking, just sit back and listen. One word, such as "cholesterol," can be a pointer to what you might need to pay attention to in your body.

Now that you're in the hologram that represents healthy organs and other body systems, ask the first layer of your field how your body is doing. Are there any problems, and if so, which area of the body are they in?

Take a few deep breaths to relax and allow your awareness to absorb any information. Remember intuitive information is delivered in a way that is neutral and not alarming. If your being registers an issue, take note of it, and thank the first layer of your aura for any data it provides. We will find out more about what may or may not be happening in your being as we go further into the scan.

Is Your Mind Wandering or Is It Intuition?

If you view or sense old memories from your past while scanning your body, don't dismiss them or think that your mind is wandering. These reminiscences could be hints of what's going on in your body or life right now. Your infinite wisdom will use images and stories that you already know from your history to communicate information that is pertinent now.

Congratulations! You have just finished scanning your first chakra, auric field, and all your organs and body systems via the hologram. Do you feel any different? Perhaps the lower half of your body feels lighter, tingles, or seems heavier. During the scan, did you become emotional? It wouldn't be unusual to have new sensations after scanning your energy because it represents so much of you, including your past, future, and parts of your life you have yet to discover.

•   •   •

Let's move on to scanning your second energy center and the second layer of the field. If you have been sitting for a while, you may want to stand up for a minute or two and stretch your body. While taking a break, rub your hands together briskly to free any stagnant energy or information that might be stored in your hands. We want to start with a clean slate before we continue.

When you return to a comfortable position, set an intention—setting the stage before beginning a new adventure charges the event with positive energy. Here are a few examples, or you can make up your own:

- As I venture into an inspection of my second chakra, may I welcome all information and increase my capacity to know all things.
- May I grow my ability to understand my energy and the energy of others, and may the experience be blissful.

To continue evaluating your being, place your non-dominant hand about one inch below your belly button, the home of your second chakra. This is the juicy chakra, where Kundalini energy emerges, and it's also the place where the second layer of the auric field is revealed. This field houses all your true emotions, which are key to unearthing your natural guidance system.

What are you feeling while visiting this area—warmth, coolness, tingling, excitement? Or are there impressions, visual or emotional, that are emerging while your hand is present with this chakra, which is a beautiful orange ball of light. Whatever you're experiencing is a clue to how your emotions flow in your body. Take note and ask this energy center, "What area of my emotional body needs to be balanced?"

It's important to have balance in our emotional body because intuitive information is felt neutrally as universal knowledge recognizes nothing as wrong or bad.

Now bring your attention to the mate of this chakra, located at the lower back. The mate houses your will in all the juicy areas of your life, career (or what you do in the world), money, partnership, creativity, and all relationships. Ask your will not to limit you in any way while you're in this space. You may notice after setting this intent that the muscles in your back relax. Freeing our will works magic in the body!

Now move your sensing wisdom beyond your body to the second layer of your auric field, which is approximately six inches away from your body. Let your being play in this more relaxed energy field, which stretches out to one foot in width and circles your body like an eggshell.

This field can be a green hue, and within it are multicolored bubbles. The effervescence of the bubbles symbolizes your emotions. Are your bubbles crashing into one another (emotional drama) or gently touching each other (awareness)? Or are your bubbles avoiding each other (emotionless)?

While perceiving this energy system, ask the field what area requires attention—home, work, body, mind, or spirit? While assessing your emotions, also ask how your reproductive organs are working. If something about your reproductive organs comes to mind, think about or visualize your ovaries, fallopian tubes, and then your uterus. If you're a man, think or visualize your testes and then your prostate. If any of the organs feel highlighted in your mind, or stand out in some other way, write them down. Now, imagine beautiful healing light moving into your reproductive organs and direct a little extra light to any area that stood out.

Remember all information is valid, so jot your findings down, even if they feel confusing in the moment. At a later date they could prove to be invaluable.

When I observe this field in my clients, I may be drawn to the green hue, but most of the time my connection is auditory. I may hear words such as, "Pay attention to their emotions regarding their family."

Release and Heal Old Emotional Pain

Everyone in the universe is doing the best they can with what they know. If during your scan you picked up on some hurt or negative feelings about a situation in your current life, or in the past, try this healing exercise my spirit guides taught me ten years ago, and which I still use today.

However negative the situation is, know that each person involved in it, including you, has a higher self. A part of themselves, with keen awareness and the ability to unconditionally love, wishes the human part of them had shown up more compassionate and loving in this particular situation and in all circumstances.

In your mind's eye, recreate a different outcome for the situation that is closer to what you want. For example, maybe when you were a child you didn't get along with your siblings. Over the years you have tried to establish a warm connection with them, but nothing seems to work. In fact, whenever you think of this (most likely too often), you feel that you don't have many close relationships.

Now imagine that you have kind and fulfilling relationships with your siblings and many friends. The closeness deeply touches your heart. You don't have to figure out how or why these relationships are healed; they just are. Maybe in your mind's eye they always have been wonderful. You can also feel how much others in your life value your friendship, advice, and companionship.

Spend about five to ten minutes a day, or a few minutes right now, feeling the outcome you have always desired. Unhealed emotions can impair your energetic system, including the second layer of your auric field. Thankfully, anything can be healed at any moment. The higher selves of every person involved in the situation will work with you to heal the pain. So let them!

(To learn more about spirit guides and the higher self, see the Frequently Asked Questions section at the end of the book, on page 177.)

• • •

Let's move on to scanning the third chakra and the third layer of your auric field. Place your non-dominant hand at the solar plexus, in the middle of your rib cage at your mid-abdomen. This is a powerful energy center because it governs your immune system and your feelings about yourself. When you think about your immunity and compassion for yourself, how does the energy in your body react? Does your energy feel solid or invisible? How does your mind react when you think about this idea? Spend a few moments feeling how your being reacts to this part of the scan. Make notes to consider later on.

Now move your awareness to the mate of the third chakra, which is located at your mid-spine. This area is about how you perceive yourself in the world. Whether you see this area, or hear, or feel it, know that it is there.

How do you see yourself in this world called Earth? Are you an active participant or do you usually sit back? Most importantly, are you in the world the way you wish to be? Each being has an accurate sense of who they really are. Most are uncomfortable with their greatest qualities and hold themselves back from experiencing them. As you sense this part of your body and energy, ask for correct sense of self to emerge. It is always with you because natural gifts and talents never go away!

Now let's visit the third layer of your auric field. It's about one and a half feet away from your body and may feel a little heavy as it houses all your thoughts. When I visit this field, I see hundreds of drawers like ones in a dresser, free-floating among thousands of grid lines of light that have a warm or light yellow energy all around the image of the drawers. In each drawer are many thoughts. When I view another's thoughts, they are usually full of negativity. After touching thousands of people, I have come to realize that most humans loathe themselves.

The first time I scanned my chakras, I couldn't see my third energy center. I literally had such little energy present in my mid-abdomen that I was unable to visualize it. Most of the disturbances related to this chakra are about self-doubt and feeling anxious because of a lack of confidence. Learning to acknowledge yourself as the amazing being that you are heals the energy here, erases negative thinking, and creates a healthier body. When you notice that the energy of your being is depleted, ask the Divine for insight about how you can heal the original wound. Remember all answers have a connection to you, because you are a part of the universe, but you may need to ask to discover it.

You Have to Ask if You Want Answers

It's important to ask questions when you assess your body, emotions, and mental or spiritual health. Many people think that the information they need just magically drops from the heavens and into their lap like a delivery from FedEx. When that doesn't happen, people tend to think that they're not connected and certainly not intuitive. But heaven needs to hear what you need directly from your mouth because most of us don't have meditative minds. Instead our heads are tied up in a knotted maze that even Houdini couldn't escape through the obstacles and make sense of it all. With mindful practice, the questions you ask will be fewer and fewer and the flow of knowledge will eventually feel like a super-fast highway, because your mind will be free to participate.

Mindfulness is the act of being centered in the present moment. It is being fully attentive to real feelings and thoughts that feed your being, soul, energy, and heart in a positive way. When mindfulness is missing from your daily life, there is a tendency to overreact to your thoughts, sending alarming energy into the body that creates unhealthy and fearful feelings, which distract us from our genuine selves and heartfelt life-path.

To learn to be mindful, pay attention to what you're doing in the moment no matter what it is. If you're washing dishes by hand, feel the suds on your fingers along with the weight of the dish. Feel the temperature of the water and notice your posture. There is so much to take in when you're focused on the present, and all of it leads to a deeper connection to the awareness you seek.

Before we leave this energy center, let's send beautiful light to the organs present here: liver, pancreas, gallbladder, spleen, stomach, and small intestines.

As you send light to each one, how does the organ take in the energy? Does it flow well? Or does the organ feel sticky or heavy and unable to let the energy flow in? Take note of your findings. If any area feels odd, send extra light to the organ while feeling love. If you have a health issues with any organ or part of your body, move inside it. You can send loving light to the area whenever you feel inspired to do so. You may soon notice improved health or become aware of a new practitioner, medicine, or natural healing supplement that creates a healthy change. This is because all healing begins with love.

• • •

Now let's move to scanning the fourth chakra and fourth layer of the auric field. Rub your hands together to clear any energy left from scanning the third chakra.

Place your non-dominant hand on the center of your chest. Take a few deep breaths and let your mind move inward, far into your body, beyond ribs, lungs, and heart muscle. As your awareness freely enters this area, you will expand into universal consciousness and unconditional love. Allow the fourth chakra to transform your energy so that you can expand into your higher frequency energy centers. The fourth chakra's energy is the basis of a shift in consciousness for the entire human race.

Let yourself go, knowing that free falling here is great for your health and wellbeing. As you surrender into the void, take note of anything that comes into your awareness. Letting go can make you feel vulnerable. Tell your being that feeling exposed is perfect and necessary in order to open yourself and detach from those things that limit you.

Scan the back of your fourth chakra, which is located in between your shoulder blades, to assess how well you're receiving energy. Record your findings, then bathe the entire area with sun-drenched light in order to charge your vibration.

Inquire about your organs in your chest cavity. Has there been a hint of change in your awareness after running sunny light there? Remember whether you hear, feel, or see it, what you're experiencing is real.

To fuse with the fourth layer of the auric field, stretch your arms out about four and a half feet away from your body to become acquainted with the fourth layer of your aura. In the depth of this amazing place, the ability exists to fully embrace everything and to realize that all exists for everyone: all love, health, wealth, and joy. Many people see the color pink when they connect here. What do you see, hear, or feel?

I see a pink color when I'm directed to pay attention to this field. It's an indicator to me that a client is overgenerous, and dedicates him or herself to others while avoiding their own needs. People who are enablers have huge, strikingly pink fourth layers in their aura. A healthy fourth layer of the field looks like a vast universe with stars, moons, and suns illuminating its depth.

Before you leave this area, repeat a mantra that rushes high frequency energy into your being to prepare you for your journey into chakras five, six, and seven.

Keep your hand on your chest and repeat out loud:

I'm grateful for any guidance that allows me to surrender to love and to whatever is in the highest good for all, in each situation that is presented to me in this lifetime.

Wonderful, you're more than halfway done with your first intensive scan. Good job!

If you have been sitting for a while, now would be a good time to stand and stretch your body.

• • •

We'll now move on to the fifth energy center, which is located in the middle of your neck. After rubbing your hands together, use your non-dominant hand to connect to the fifth chakra, the highest personal power chakra in the human body. With this chakra, you may not want to put your hands directly on your throat. The weight of your hand may irritate the area. Generally, I place my hand just slightly above the area, maybe about half an inch to one inch away from my skin.

Notice how your body feels when your energy is present with this vortex. How do your jaw, mouth, teeth, and gums feel? Do you notice any temperature changes? How is your stress level? Has it calmed down in comparison to how you felt before exploring the fifth chakra, or has it escalated?

Now bring your attention to the back of your neck, where the cervical vertebrae live. How is your neck feeling in this moment? If you typically have neck pain, are you noticing an improvement in your symptoms, or is your neck all of a sudden feeling uncomfortable? Take note of your discoveries.

This chakra is so sensitive that most people can feel even the slightest shift in its energy when they become mindful of it. Throughout your day, this chakra is reacting to how you speak your truth. It feels fantastic when you do, and not so great when you don't.

Now bring your awareness to your thyroid gland. It spreads across the trachea like a butterfly. Holistic practitioners believe this gland works overtime to balance other endocrine glands when they are having difficulty performing their duties. Let's send wise and stunning light to the thyroid gland and any other part of this area that needs energy. Sending light to the thyroid gland will help your entire endocrine system balance even if you take medication for the gland.

To connect with your aura and the fifth layer of its field, reach your hand out about five and a half feet. If your arm can't reach that far, just imagine that you have made contact with it, because intention is everything.

Connecting to this field with the optimistic intention of encountering your life purpose is as empowering and life altering as speaking your truth. The energy of all your natural gifts and talents dwells in this field. When you express yourself honestly, the fifth chakra electrifies the field and so makes the real *you* detectable.

When I'm guided to this field, I see the color blue with hundreds of silver-colored grid lines lacing through it. The blue color of the field is usually similar to the shade of blue of the person's fifth chakra. Shades of color in the body can vary depending on the person's well-being, thoughts, and ability to release stagnant energy.

When a person is getting ready to realize their potential, I'm shown pictures in the fifth layer of their natural talents and blessed abilities. What are you sensing right now?

As we prepare to leave this area, here is a prayer to repeat as an affirmation of your truth:

Every day and in every way
I ask to recognize and cherish my truth.

Your body might be buzzing right now, because you're energetically merging with high vibration chakras.

. . .

After rubbing your hands together, place your non-dominant hand on your forehead to connect with the third eye. Examining this energy center can be thrilling, especially since you've been building your intuitive muscle during this scan.

Bring all your attention to your head and the amazing chakra there. Whether you have been aware of it or not, your ability to connect to the insights that are housed here has always been yours. Take a few deep breaths and a moment to own this natural birthright.

Ask out loud, "How can I best receive and understand my symbolic language to see, hear, and feel clearly?" Take notes on whatever comes to mind.

Now use your scanning abilities to assess the neurotransmitters in your brain. These tiny devices speedily share data based on your beliefs throughout your central nervous system. When they broadcast the data, the neurotransmitters start chemical responses that create emotions to support your beliefs. As a part of your assessment, inventory the common themes of your beliefs—what you think about you and your life. Here is a list of words to help you identify them:

- happiness
- poverty
- bliss
- fear
- gratitude

- riches
- envy
- peace
- victimization
- love

- anger
- intelligence
- omnipresent
- crazy
- balance

Pick four of these words that seem to fit your thoughts. Don't judge the words or yourself in this process; the ability to be clairvoyant, clairaudient, or clairsentient comes through supreme acceptance of yourself and everyone else.

Direct precious love and light to all your emotions and beliefs while setting the intention that they support you in positive ways. Great! Now keep the light shining into all your brain matter, glands, and senses. How do they feel? What colors or impressions are you receiving? Write them down or take a mental note of them.

Now try to measure the length of the front mate of your third eye. It can extend to approximately one foot straight out in front of your forehead. No matter its length, imagine that it's deeply purple and energetically stretches into the fourth dimension: the psychic realm. Whether you see it, hear it, or feel it, know that it is there.

Bring your attention to the back mate of this chakra and imagine that realm of all-knowing, the fourth dimension, is a great and close friend of yours. The well-being and love you can feel there surpasses any other. Allow this back mate to absorb all the love that it can into your consciousness.

Expand your awareness out to the sixth layer of your aura (about six and a half feet away from you) and open yourself to this omnipresent field that judges nothing and can see utter greatness in all things and all beings. As you feel its presence, ask to be given the most expansive awareness possible.

Connecting to this auric field will help you understand the workings of the human mind, and give you insight into the reasons why we do the things we do. This will fill your being with utter compassion for all our choices.

While basking within the sixth layer of your field, how does it represent itself to you? When I initially connect to this field, I see a deep purple color, but as I engage with it, I'm transported into deep space. It looks dark and mysterious, but I feel completely safe and vastly curious about everything around me. What do you sense?

Take a deep breath and appreciate your dedication to your body as we prepare for your final destination—the seventh energy center!

● ● ●

Bring all your attention to the top of your head where the seventh vortex is located. Rub your hands together and take a few deep breaths to move energy in your body, then breathe out to release anything that is no longer serving you.

This chakra can extend many feet and even many miles outside of your body. The chakra grows upward as you cultivate your spirituality and raise your awareness, leading you to understand the truth that you are an irreplaceable part of creation.

Stretch out your non-dominant arm and feel this massive structure. Can you feel it? How does it present itself to you? What color do you see there and what messages can you hear from this enchanted vortex? Whatever you see, hear, or feel is perfect and real. Write it down.

While you're having this brilliant realization, scan your nervous system that is outside of your brain for any issues, signs, or messages. How does your nervous system feel? Is it alive and active? How is the integrity of your skin? If you notice anything out of order, send healing light to the areas and thank the universe for your wholeness.

Now mindfully reach out to the seventh layer of the field. This enormous field is the final layer of your aura. This field shows you that all energy expands forever because there is no end or beginning to the universe. Everything exists always and forever. Let the field show you in the best way for you how nothing ends. Take a few deep breaths and release old ideas and inhale new spacious ones.

How do you make out this field? What do you hear, see, or feel? Dance with your symbols and breathe in your individuation.

For me, this field is a bright gold color, full of trillions of grid lines of blinding light. Connecting to this field helps you to understand that the universe can see, hear, and feel your magnificent being with absolute certainty.

Before we leave your chakras and aura, let's send light from this amazing field to your whole energetic system to seal up any leaks that may be present. Sometimes energy fields can become fatigued and leak out vital life-force energy. Set an intention that your intuition knows exactly where these leaks are, and that the blinding light from this field and from creation will instantly transform them into healthy vigor. Take a few final minutes to bathe in this energy of well-being.

Congratulations! You have finished your first thorough scan of your energy system. May each day inspire you to know and love every vibration you are!

Appendix

Chakra Reference Table

First Chakra: First Family	
Color	Red
Location	Perineum
Emotional Health	Your capacity to heal your relationship with your first family
Diseases	Rheumatoid arthritis and degenerative joint disease; blood, bone, colon, and rectal cancers; colon and blood disorders; musculoskeletal problems with the knees, hamstrings, and all ligaments and tendons from the hips to the toes; hemorrhoids, sciatica, and sickle-cell anemia
Exercises	See the exercises at the end of chapter 2.
	Mantra: Every day I realize the real beauty of my family and celebrate our unique qualities.
	Repeat mantra for a few minutes a day to open your awareness to what you need to know about your childhood.

Second Chakra: Passion

Color	Orange
Location	Just below the navel
Emotional Health	Your capacity to feel great joy
Diseases	Ovarian, cervical, uterine, prostate, bladder, and kidney cancers; ectopic pregnancy, endometriosis, and all other reproductive problems; renal failure; adrenal disease; lower back pain; appendicitis; ruptured discs in lumbar area
Exercises	See the exercises at the end of chapter 3. Mantra: Thank you for the joy that fills my being every day. Repeat mantra each day, preferably upon waking, to help you identify joyful things or situations throughout the day.

Third Chakra: Self-Love

Color	Yellow
Location	Solar plexus
Emotional Health	Your capacity to feel self-love
Diseases	Chronic fatigue syndrome, lupus, diabetes, chemical sensitivities, scleroderma, diverticulitis, stomach cancer, and acid reflux; musculoskeletal problems in the mid-spine; celiac, Crohn's, Lyme, and inflammatory bowel diseases; diseases of the connective tissue, liver, pancreas, gallbladder, and spleen
Exercises	See the exercises at the end of chapter 4. Mantra: Every day, in every way, I acknowledge my self-worth. Repeat mantra two or three times a day, even silently, to begin valuing yourself.

Fourth Chakra: Universal Love	
Color	Green
Location	Center of the chest
Emotional Health	Your capacity to give and receive universal love
Diseases	Breast cancer; carpal tunnel syndrome; thoracic outlet syndrome; diseases of the heart, lung, lymphatic system, thymus gland, and circulatory system; musculoskeletal problems with the upper back
Exercises	See exercises at the end of chapter 5. Mantra: Each day I move toward greater balance in my ability to give and receive universal love. Repeating this mantra can serve as a prayer. Repeat in the morning and evening.

Fifth Chakra: Speaking Truth	
Color	Blue
Location	Throat
Emotional Health	Your capacity to speak your truth
Diseases	Musculoskeletal problems with the neck and cervical discs; diseases or disorders of the mouth, tongue, and larynx, including thyroid cancer; periodontal disease, gingivitis, and tonsillitis; problems with speech, swallowing, or sense of taste
Exercises	See the exercises at the end of chapter 6. Mantra: Expressing my truth feels natural and empowers me to be more of who I am. Repeat daily for one minute to ensure that you express your needs and ask great questions. This mantra is especially helpful in calming yourself before a difficult conversation.

Sixth Chakra: Intuition	
Color	Indigo
Location	Center of your brain
Emotional Health	Your capacity to trust your intuition
Diseases	Diseases and disorders of the brain, including Alzheimer's disease, dementia, brain tumors, migraines, headaches, and vertigo; hearing disorders, including tinnitus, ear infections, and hearing loss; seeing disorders and diseases, including glaucoma, cataracts, and vision problems; diseases of the sinus, including infections and deviated septum.
Exercises	See the exercises at the end of chapter 7. Mantra: Embracing my intuition is one of my greatest joys. Repeat mantra for several minutes as you fall asleep to more quickly integrate its meaning into your subconscious and conscious mind.

Seventh Chakra: Spirit	
Color	White
Location	Crown of the head
Emotional Health	Your capacity to connect to spirit
Diseases	Diseases of the nervous and peripheral nervous systems, including ALS (Lou Gehrig's disease); Guillain-Barré syndrome; multiple sclerosis; neoplasm; pain sensitivity; diseases of the skin, including psoriasis, eczema, alopecia, contact dermatitis, hives, and vitiligo
Exercises	See the exercises at the end of chapter 8. Mantra: Spirit and I are one. Repeat this mantra daily while doing something to celebrate your joyful connection, such as dancing around the house with candles lit.

* NOTE: *Some diseases are associated with more than one chakra.*

Frequently Asked Questions

1. What is a chakra?

   A chakra is an energy center located in all living things. It's shaped like a cone or vortex, and spins in a clockwise direction when you look at the face of the cone. It receives and transmits energy.

2. What is clairsentience?

   Clairsentience means to feel deeply within our world and beyond. An example would be the ability of psychometry, which is when someone is able to touch an object and receive information about its history simply by that touch.

3. What is clairaudience?

   Clairaudience is to deeply hear in our world almost to the point of annoying sensitivity to earth sounds. It is also the ability to hear outside of our world. An example might be hearing the voices of angels or the music in heaven.

4. What is clairvoyance?

   Clairvoyance is the ability to see deeply into our world and beyond, perhaps visualizing microorganisms without a microscope or see beings who live on the other side.

5. What is energy medicine?
Energy medicine is a general term used to describe a wide and ever changing field of holistic healing, based on working with the human energy system to help heal disease.

6. What is intuitive healing?
Intuitive healing encompasses a deep sense of knowing in one's being to assess and collect awareness of what can heal us.

7. What is the higher self?
The higher self is the representation of your soul in its fullness. It exists somewhere outside of your body, but relatively close so that you can access it.

8. What is the psychic realm?
The psychic realm is also referred to as the astral plane. It is a dimensional time-space reality connected to earth where intuitive, psychic, and past-life information can be accessed.

9. What is an aura?
An aura is an organized mass of energy that surrounds the human body.

10. What is intuition?
Intuition means to receive and understand information beyond the five senses.

11. What are grid lines?
Grid lines are beings of light that move throughout the universe and into everything that exists, in organized, linear lines. Some believe grid lines are what hold the universe together.

12. What is grounding?
    Grounding is the ability to connect to earth and
    use its life-giving energy to sustain your human
    existence.

13. What does it mean to be a multisensory being?
    A multisensory being doesn't rely solely on its
    intelligence, but on its ability to connect to the
    intelligence of the universe. In doing so, it learns
    and advances its consciousness quickly.

14. What is a vortex?
    A vortex is a rotating, cone-shaped substance that is
    completely energetic. The words vortex and chakra
    are interchangeable.

15. What are the chakras in the palms of one's hand?
    The chakras in the palms of the hand are the
    only medium-sized chakras in the body. They are
    approximately an inch in diameter. They allow
    healing energy to move through them and absorb
    stagnant energy to be recycled.

16. What are the chakras in the feet?
    The chakras in each foot are part of the 3,000
    smaller chakras present in joints, muscle mass, and
    subcutaneous tissue. The small chakras also make
    up the meridian lines and acupressure points.

17. What are spirit guides?
    Spirit guides are beings that live on the other side
    (another dimension outside of the earth plane where
    we travel to after we leave this world). Their job
    is to guide you while you live a life here on Earth.
    Before you incarnated to Earth, you asked beings,
    whom you believe are more evolved than you are,
    to guide you. Those who agreed are now your

spirit guides. Their dedication and love for you is un-measurable and unconditional.

Further Reading

Cartier, Aimee Colette. *Getting Answers: Using Your Intuition to Discover Your Best Life*. Vashon, WA: Spreading Blessing Media, 2010.

Dooley, Mike. *Infinite Possibilities: The Art of Living Your Dreams*. New York, NY: Simon and Schuster, 2009.

Fortson, Leigh. *Embrace, Release, Heal*. Boulder, CO: Sounds True, Inc., 2011.

Hicks, Esther and Jerry Hicks. *The Vortex: Where the Law of Attraction Assembles All Cooperative Relationships*. Carlsbad, CA: Hay House, Inc., 2009.

Hover-Kramer, Dorothea. *Healing Touch*. Boulder, CO: Sounds True, Inc., 2011.

MacLeod, Ainslie. *The Transformation: Healing Your Past Lives to Realize Your Soul's Potential*. Boulder, CO: Sounds True, Inc., 2010.

Muller, Robert. *Most of All They Taught Me Happiness*. Los Angeles, CA: Amare Media LLC., 2005.

Rodegast, Pat and Judith Stanton. *Emmanuel's Book: A Manual for Living Comfortably in the Cosmos*. New York, NY: Bantam Books, 1987.

Singer, Michael. *The Untethered Soul: The Journey Beyond Yourself*. Oakland, CA: New Harbinger Productions, Inc., 2007.

Tolle, Eckhart. *The Power of Now*. Novato, CA: New World Publishing, 1999.

Truman, Karol K. *Feelings Buried Alive Never Die*. Brigham City, UT: Brigham Distributing, 1991.

Zukav, Gary. *The Seat of the Soul*. New York, NY: Simon and Schuster, 1999.

In Loving Memory of Tom

TOM, WHOSE STORY I TELL in chapter 2, passed away during the production of this book. In the final days of his life, he was surrounded in love by his wife, children, sisters, and other extended family members. During that time, he expressed his peace, curiosity for his next adventure, and gratitude for the extra time he had here on Earth. Tom, I wish you an amazing journey. You will be missed by many.

About the Author

MARIE MANUCHEHRI, RN, IS A nationally known energy intuitive. Marie bridges conventional medicine and holistic healing to help people release pain, heal their wounds, and emerge into expanded consciousness. Her energy medicine practice began twelve years ago, when she was working as an oncology nurse and discovered the energetic relationship between health and disease.

Marie's private practice, which grew by word of mouth, now includes thousands of clients from across the world. She is a sought-after public speaker and teacher, and she runs a mentoring program for others interested in the field of energy medicine. Her bi-weekly radio show, *Where Energy and Medicine Meet,* on KKNW 1150AM in Seattle, Washington, also streamed live via the Internet, is wildly popular. *Intuitive Self-Healing* is her first book. She lives in Kirkland, Washington. For more information, visit her website: energyintuitive.com.

About the Illustrator

SUSAN RUSSELL HALL IS A painter and medical illustrator who has documented more than 6,500 surgeries from life in the operating room.

Hall's medical drawings have been published in more than thirty books and journals and have been used in professional and educational presentations internationally. Her encaustic paintings have been exhibited in more than sixty solo or group shows.

Hall was one of forty artists selected to be included in the seventh International Biennial Exhibition, Encaustic Works 2009 in New York. Her work resides in many collections, including the Tacoma Art Museum, Cairncross & Hemplemann (a Seattle law firm), and MultiCare Hospital in Tacoma, Washington.

About Sounds True

SOUNDS TRUE IS A MULTIMEDIA publisher whose mission is to inspire and support personal transformation and spiritual awakening. Founded in 1985 and located in Boulder, Colorado, we work with many of the leading spiritual teachers, thinkers, healers, and visionary artists of our time. We strive with every title to preserve the essential "living wisdom" of the author or artist. It is our goal to create products that not only provide information to a reader or listener, but that also embody the quality of a wisdom transmission.

For those seeking genuine transformation, Sounds True is your trusted partner. At SoundsTrue.com you will find a wealth of free resources to support your journey, including exclusive weekly audio interviews, free downloads, interactive learning tools, and other special savings on all our titles.

To watch a bonus video with author Marie Manuchehri, and listen to a podcast interview with Marie and Sounds True publisher Tami Simon, please visit SoundsTrue.com/bonus/IntuitiveHealing.